About Pfeiffer

Pfeiffer serves the professional development and hands-on resource needs of training and human resource practitioners and gives them products to do their jobs better. We deliver proven ideas and solutions from experts in HR development and HR management, and we offer effective and customizable tools to improve workplace performance. From novice to seasoned professional, Pfeiffer is the source you can trust to make yourself and your organization more successful.

 **Essential Knowledge** Pfeiffer produces insightful, practical, and comprehensive materials on topics that matter the most to training and HR professionals. Our Essential Knowledge resources translate the expertise of seasoned professionals into practical, how-to guidance on critical workplace issues and problems. These resources are supported by case studies, worksheets, and job aids and are frequently supplemented with CD-ROMs, websites, and other means of making the content easier to read, understand, and use.

Essential Tools Pfeiffer's Essential Tools resources save time and expense by offering proven, ready-to-use materials—including exercises, activities, games, instruments, and assessments—for use during a training or team-learning event. These resources are frequently offered in looseleaf or CD-ROM format to facilitate copying and customization of the material.

Pfeiffer also recognizes the remarkable power of new technologies in expanding the reach and effectiveness of training. While e-hype has often created whizbang solutions in search of a problem, we are dedicated to bringing convenience and enhancements to proven training solutions. All our e-tools comply with rigorous functionality standards. The most appropriate technology wrapped around essential content yields the perfect solution for today's on-the-go trainers and human resource professionals.

Pfeiffer
www.pfeiffer.com

Essential resources for training and HR professionals

D1530570

25 ACTIVITIES FOR DEVELOPING TEAM LEADERS

Fran Rees

Pfeiffer
www.pfeiffer.com

About This Book

Why is this topic important?

Teamwork continues to be one of the most important needs in organizations today. Along with effective communication and conflict management, the subject of teamwork rises again and again as a critical one. Without effective team leadership, teams do not function very well. Because team leadership requires methods and skills different from traditional management, it is important that team leaders receive adequate training.

What can you achieve with this resource?

If you are a manager or organization leader, a trainer, a consultant, a facilitator, or someone responsible for training team leaders, this book will be a resource for you. The training activities can be used separately from one another as needed, or some of them can be selected and delivered as a training program in several units. They can be delivered in short time frames, targeted to particular audiences, and, in some cases, repeated for further development of the same participants.

How is this resource organized?

The training activities in this book are organized around the L.E.A.D. model of leadership from *How to LEAD Work Teams: Facilitation Skills,* by Fran Rees. Each segment of the model is supported with several activities, and an introductory section covers overall concepts of team leadership. Each activity is a complete, stand-alone activity in itself, and all activities relate to and build on one another. It is not expected that all of the activities will be used for a particular audience, but that activities will be selected based on audience need and organization goals and constraints.

CONTENTS

ACKNOWLEDGMENTS

I WOULD LIKE TO THANK the following people for their help in the writing and production of this book: Martin Delahoussaye for his ideas and support in scoping out the book; Susan Rachmeler for her insightful and thorough comments on the manuscript; Kathleen Dolan Davies and Dawn Kilgore for their usual calm and efficient support in the many details of producing the book; other consultants and trainers for their prior work in designing group activities and from whose work some of the exercises were adapted; the reviewers who made suggestions for improving the manuscript; and my daughter Lauren and husband David, who keep me encouraged as I write. Thanks to all of you for your help and support.

Introduction

Purpose of the Book

THE PURPOSE OF THIS BOOK is to provide trainers, consultants, and those responsible for developing team leaders with a modular package of activities geared to building team leader skills and knowledge. It is designed to allow maximum flexibility in delivery, while providing trainers with a range of activities that cover a broad scope of team leader topics and issues. Each activity calls for a skilled facilitator to structure and lead the process and to facilitate discussions.

Rationale for the Book

The environment of many organizations requires a large number of teams and team leaders. Many organizations rely heavily on the work of small teams (from five to fifteen members) to accomplish much of the work. In the fast-paced, real world of today's organizations, individuals are frequently expected to take charge and put together informal, short-lived teams to solve problems or accomplish segments of the work. On some teams, several or all of the members may be expected to lead the team from time to time.

As a training and development consultant for the past twenty years, I have worked with teams, team leaders, managers, project leaders, specialists in their field, and cross-functional teams. In working with these groups and individuals, I have served in a variety of capacities, including team member, team leader, manager, trainer, consultant, training designer, and, most frequently, facilitator. From these years of experience and various vantage points, I have come to understand the critical importance of team leadership in most organizational endeavors, both large and small.

Without the specific skills, expertise, and dedication of a good leader, a group often runs into trouble. Miscommunication, unresolved differences of opinion, interpersonal conflict, lack of direction, lack of cooperation, and other problems plague teams without adequate leadership. Without a leader who knows how to draw on both individual and group expertise, teams frequently rely on the drive and dominance of one or a few members, leaving others uninvolved, disgruntled, or under-contributing.

Due to the pace and demands made on workers in today's organizations, training of team leaders is difficult. It often takes too much time and money to pull people out of work and train them adequately. Those needing team leader training may not even be identified until they are faced with having to lead a team. As mentioned above, people are often expected to take on a team leadership role as part of their job, whether they have team leadership training or not.

The activities in this book were selected and designed to fit the needs of busy organizations. They give organizations the chance to tailor the length, timing, and subject matter of training to best fit the environment. Many of them take no more than two hours to complete. They can be spread over a reasonable period of time and will take team leaders away from their jobs for only short periods of time. Trainers can strategize to get the most from these activities. Using them to train team leaders provides sound training and allows flexibility to select the topics and skills most appropriate for each audience and each environment.

Selecting several of the activities and training a group of team leaders over a reasonable (but not too drawn-out) period of time can bring about many benefits for team leaders and the organization. Team leaders receive support, knowledge, and skills to do their work more effectively and gain new insight from others in the sessions. They are given time away from the stress of work to contemplate their roles and responsibilities and to develop effective leadership methods and skills; this, in turn, gives them added confidence on the job. Sharing problems, challenges, and concerns with other participants connects team leaders to those with similar roles, and this connection builds morale and provides camaraderie.

When participants come from the same organization, there is the added benefit of shaping the team leadership in that organization. When participants come from different organizations, the benefit is the crossover of ideas and sharing of new methods and information. Because they call for ample interaction and team-based activities, these activities provide the added benefit of building a team spirit in the participant group. In many of the activities, participants identify strategies and tips for dealing with team leader issues and challenges they are currently facing on the job.

Scope and Content

This book will work within the constraints of today's busy organizations. First, each activity can be used independently, yet all activities are harmonious with one another; in other words, each activity can be used as a stand-alone training unit or grouped with other activities. Some or all of the activities can be used, leaving the trainer with a wide range of options for customizing training to fit a particular audience.

Second, each activity can be conducted in from 1 1/2 to 4 hours, which allows trainers to deliver meaningful training with minimal interruption of work.

Third, the activities cover the full spectrum of team leadership skills and are designed around the L.E.A.D. model of team leadership (see page 5) put forth in *How to Lead Work Teams: Facilitation Skills* (Rees, 2001):

Lead with a clear purpose

Empower people to participate

Aim for consensus

Direct the process

The book is divided into five sections, a section on team leadership followed by one section for each segment of the model, with several activities in each section. There is, therefore, a balance of activities to support the basic concepts and major skill areas of team leadership: defining purpose and vision, eliciting full participation, building consensus, and directing the process of teamwork and development.

Activities in Section 1 cover the subject of team leadership and lay the foundation for the use of the L.E.A.D. model. Exercises and discussions in these activities help team leaders develop a workable philosophy of team leadership and explore their own ideas about how to function effectively as a team leader.

Section 2 activities cover the subject of leading a team with purpose and clarity. Exercises and discussions in these activities help team leaders develop the ability to focus the team, set clear team goals, prepare a results-oriented meeting, and keep the team energized with a sense of purpose.

Activities in Section 3 help team leaders with the skills and attitudes necessary to draw out the full participation of team members. Activities in this section are designed to build the leadership skills of remaining neutral, multi-level listening, asking questions, recording and clarifying people's ideas and inputs, and facilitating meetings that maximize team member participation and focus on results.

Section 4 activities focus on tools and techniques team leaders need to lead a group to consensus. This section builds understanding of what consensus is and is not, the value of consensus, and when not to seek consensus. It also builds skills in team leaders to help teams avoid, manage, and work through conflict. Several consensus tools are presented in this section.

Section 5 activities focus team leaders on the steps and processes involved in team leadership. Working through these exercises will help team leaders sort out where the team is in its development, work, and life as a team. These activities help give scope, order, and direction to the overall process of leading a team, as well as assist the team leader in dealing with common team challenges.

Activities are further designated as Beginning (I), Intermediate (II), or Advanced (III); this designation is to help trainers and managers deliver training that best meets the needs of their audience. *Beginning* level activities build foundational skills, *intermediate* level activities build further on those basic skills, and *advanced* level activities focus on difficult situations team leaders face and how to deal with them.

An Overview of Activities matrix has been provided on page 8 to assist trainers in selecting and sequencing the activities in this book. Based on the needs of the audience and the constraints placed on training in the way of time, budget, and space, trainers can design a training program to fit a particular group.

How to Use This Book

First, familiarize yourself with the contents of the book. Next, read the "Managing the Group Training Session" later in the Introduction to understand your role and tasks as a trainer/facilitator for these activities. Then read through the introductory portion of each activity to understand the scope, content, goals, and supporting exercises. Use the Overview of Activities matrix on page 8 to review the activities in relation to level of difficulty, skills and concepts covered, and purpose of the activity.

L.E.A.D. Model

Leader Functions	Group Needs Met	Leader Tasks	Team-Member Tasks
Lead with a clear purpose	• Common goals • Attention to content • Leadership	• Set boundaries • Interpret company goals • Facilitate team's setting of its goals • Evaluate and track progress toward goals	• Ask questions to test own understanding • Participate in setting goals for team • Help leader track and evaluate progress toward goals
Empower to participate	• High levels of involvement of all members • Maintenance of self-esteem • Leadership • Respect for differences • Trust	• Ask questions • Listen • Show understanding • Summarize • Seek divergent viewpoints • Record ideas	• Contribute ideas from own experience and knowledge • Listen to others • Build on others' ideas • Consider others' ideas • Ask questions • Think creatively
Aim for consensus	• Constructive conflict resolution • Power within group to make decisions • Leadership • Trust	• Use group-process techniques (brainstorming, problem solving, prioritization, etc.) • Ask questions • Listen • Seek common interests • Summarize • Confront in a constructive way	• Focus on common interests and goals • Listen to and consider others' ideas • Make own needs known • Disagree in a constructive way
Direct the process	• Attention to process • Leadership • Trust	• Give clear directions • Intervene to keep group on track • Read group and adjust • Remain neutral • Suggest alternate processes to help group achieve goal	• Listen • Keep purpose in mind • Stay focused on objective • Use own energy and enthusiasm to help process along

Select any activities that are appropriate for the people you will be training. If you are designing a team leader training program using several of the exercises, select activities from all of the sections to balance out the topics covered. Here are some suggested approaches to selecting activities:

- Assess the needs and skill levels of those being trained (work with someone who knows the group, if possible). Review the activities and pick and choose which ones best meet the needs of the group.

- Meet with the group being trained and ask them to select which training they most need, based on the Overview of Activities matrix.

- Lead one or two activities to get an idea of the skill level of your group. Then select other appropriate activities.

- Select the basic activities and offer them as training. Then let participants select which additional sessions to attend.

- Use the Overview of Activities matrix to design a training program based on the needs of your group.

- Offer basic, intermediate, and advanced level training to select audiences based on their needs.

The Overview of Activities

Use the Overview of Activities in this section to help you review the activities at a glance and determine the level of learning for each one. Levels of learning are designated as beginning (I), intermediate (II), and advanced (III). The activities labeled intermediate and advanced build on skills and knowledge gained from the beginning activities. However, it is not necessary to train team leaders in all of the beginning activities before doing intermediate level activities. Nor do the advanced activities have to follow all of the intermediate ones. These are simply rough guidelines to help in selecting the training.

Understanding the Trainer's Code

A "Trainer's Code" is included in the Overview of Activities to give you an idea of the level of trainer/facilitator skills and experience required to lead the activity. A "low" level of difficulty requires basic facilitator skills and moderate experience. A "medium" level of difficulty requires a higher level of facilitator skills (for example, the ability to facilitate a lively discussion and accurately record key points made) and more experience as a facilitator. A "high" level of difficulty requires not only strong facilitator skills, but also the ability to think on one's feet and to keep the group on track during more controversial or complex exercises or discussions.

However, as is true for all training and facilitating, each situation will differ depending on the group dynamics, on what the participants bring to the session (experience level, attitude, work and personal pressures, etc.), and on the work environment surrounding the training session. When looking at the difficulty designation, keep in mind that other things may impact your ability to facilitate the session smoothly, such as the size or type of group, the "mood/attitude" of the group as a whole, the environments group members come from, and/or the training environment (this includes the time of day of the session, the room setup, whether or not refreshments are provided, the length of the session, and so on).

An activity designated as low difficulty, or relatively easy to lead, might not actually be so. On the other hand, one that is marked high, or more difficult to facilitate, may actually go smoothly and cause little difficulty, due to a particularly easy to facilitate group of people or other factors. *It is best to read over the activity carefully, imagining what might occur during the actual session and to imagine a few "what if" scenarios.* Certain challenges may be avoided simply by the way the session is set up, how participants are selected, the time of day the activity is offered, and so on. It is also a good idea to prepare all activities thoroughly and not to expect that they will go one way or another. Be prepared to think on your feet and to continue through the activity until all exercises and discussions have been completed. What may go a little roughly for a while may smooth out later, leaving everyone with a good experience. Activities that go too smoothly may not make much of an impression. Be careful not to judge the success of an activity too quickly. Rely on the feedback from participants at the end of the session, and give yourself a day or so to evaluate the session objectively, especially after you have had a good rest.

It is *not* intended that *all* of these activities will be used with a particular group, even though they could be since they are not redundant, but complement one another. They are designed so that you, the trainer, can select appropriate activities for a particular group of team leaders at a particular time. However, if you wish to create full-blown training programs using these activities, following are two suggestions for grouping the activities into training "units." The Team Leader Quick Start Program is a series of activities that will give team leaders a quick grounding in teams. The Facilitative Leadership for Team Leaders is a series of activities to give team leaders an understanding of facilitative leadership and a basic foundation in facilitation skills. Deliver the activities in the order shown here.

Overview of Activities

Learning Level Designations: I = Beginning; II = Intermediate; III = Advanced

Trainer's Code: Level of training/facilitating skills and experience required: Low; Medium; High.

Number	Title	Learning Level	Concepts	Purpose of the Activity	Trainer's Code
1	Leadership Style Questionnaire	II	Controlling versus facilitating style of leadership	Build philosophy of team leadership	Low
2	L.E.A.D. Bingo	I	Understanding the L.E.A.D. model	Receive examples of facilitative leadership in action	Low
3	Teamwork Step-by-Step	III	Step-by-step approach to leading a team	Learn a ten-step process for leading a team	High
4	What Teams Need	I	What must be in place for teams to succeed	Identify actions team leaders can take to meet team needs	Medium
5	Leadership Values Auction	II	How leaders' values may shift depending on the situation	Help team leaders clarify personal leadership values	High
6	Writing a Team Mission Statement	II	Criteria for a good mission; how to develop a mission	Experience a process for creating a team mission statement	Medium
7	Establishing Team Norms	I	Why norms are important; how to develop them	Observe and identify team norms in operation	Medium
8	Results-Oriented Meetings	II	Importance of setting clear meeting objectives	Give team leaders practice in writing and evaluating meeting objectives	Medium
9	Team Roles: Using the Affinity Diagram	II	Understanding team roles and responsibilities	Define team roles; experience using the Affinity Diagram	Medium
10	Good Team Meetings Don't Just Happen	I	What makes an effective team meeting	Distinguish among *vital, harmful,* and *style-related* facilitation techniques	Medium
11	Checklist for Planning a Team Meeting: A Brainstorming Process	I	How to plan for an effective meeting	Receive a checklist for planning a meeting; experience the brainstorming process	Medium
12	Questioning Skills for Team Leaders	I	Importance of knowing how to ask questions	Learn when to use open and closed questions	Medium

Overview of Activities *(continued)*

Number	Title	Learning Level	Concepts	Purpose of the Activity	Trainer's Code
13	Multi-Level Listening: A Leadership Skill	III	Four ways to listen and why they are important	Develop skill in multi-level listening	High
14	Using Group Memory in Team Meetings	II	What "group memory" is and why it is important	Practice recording "group memory"	Medium
15	Facilitation Practice for Team Leaders	III	Verbal and nonverbal skills for facilitators	Identify and practice a variety of verbal and nonverbal skills	High
16	Reaching Consensus One-on-One	I	Process for reaching consensus with another person	Practice and receive feedback on consensus-seeking skills	Medium
17	Guidelines for Reaching Consensus	II	Define consensus; identify what helps and hinders consensus	Think about what is true/false about consensus and what helps/hinders consensus	Medium
18	Consensus Techniques for Team Leaders	I	How to create an atmosphere for consensus building	Receive feedback on consensus-seeking behaviors and processes	Medium
19	Resolving Conflict: A Consensus Process	III	How team leaders can help teams resolve conflict	Use a specific process to resolve a conflict (role play)	High
20	Understanding the Stages of Team Development	I	Groups tend to develop in pre-dictable stages	Identify the characteristics of each stage	Low
21	Team Leader's Role in the Stages of Team Development	III	Team leader's role varies from stage to stage	Determine helpful team leader roles and actions for each stage	Medium
22	Feedback Aware-ness: Skill Building for Team Leaders	II	Importance of giving and receiving feedback	Practice giving and receiving feedback	High
23	Solving Team Leader Challenges	All Levels	Collaboration helps solve team leader challenges	Experience a process for solving team leader challenges	Medium
24	Evaluating Team Health	II	Understand the value of team self-evaluations	Learn how to conduct a team self-evaluation	High
25	Managing Growth of a Team Leader	II and III	Team leaders can conduct self-evaluations and target areas for growth	Receive a questionnaire and a step-by-step process to manage the growth of a team leader	Medium

**A Team Leader Quick Start Program
(basic training for new team leaders)**

Activity 2:   L.E.A.D. Bingo
Activity 7:   Establishing Team Norms
Activity 8:   Results-Oriented Meetings
Activity 9:   Team Roles: Using the Affinity Diagram
Activity 17:   Guidelines for Reaching Consensus
Activity 20:   Understanding the Stages of Team Development

**Facilitative Leadership for Team Leaders
(builds basic facilitation and meeting leadership skills)**

Activity 1:   Leadership Style Questionnaire
Activity 10:   Good Team Meetings Don't Just Happen
Activity 12:   Questioning Skills for Team Leaders
Activity 13:   Multi-Level Listening: A Leadership Skill
Activity 14:   Using Group Memory in Team Meetings
Activity 15:   Facilitation Practice for Team Leaders

Justifying the Training

Getting team leader training to those who need it may present quite a challenge. Team leaders work in demanding, dynamic, and often frustrating environments. Organizations need trained team leaders, but they face the conflict of needing team leaders on the front lines at work and needing team leaders who are well-trained.

Part of training others is selling the benefits of the training to those who have to make the decision of whom, what, and when to train. As a trainer and/or person responsible for team leader training, prepare a brief presentation that enumerates the benefits and strategies of this type of training. As you become aware of advantages and benefits, make a note of them. Record and use positive comments from the participants in your sessions to add to your presentation. Ask enthusiastic participants to come with you when you present the rationale of this type of training to decision makers.

Some of the activities call for role play and skill practice. In some activities fictitious, but realistic, case studies are used, and in other activities participants select the topics for discussion and skill practice. Be prepared to explain to those who make training decisions that these role plays and skill practice, although they take time, are extremely valuable and proven methods of learning. It is one thing to think about a concept and understand it; *it is quite another thing to change firmly ingrained patterns of thinking and behavior.* The best way to move from mental understanding to actual implementation and permanent behavioral change is to *practice that change* in simulated and real-world settings. For example, most people understand conceptually the value of a facilitator remaining neutral and recording the content of people's ideas without interjecting his or her own reactions or opinions. However, many people have difficulty actually doing this. In Activity 15, participants practice remaining neutral while leading a discussion and receive feedback from participants and the trainer on their skills. Taking the time to have each participant practice facilitation skills is a critical part of learning, and, over the years, this activity (and this type of practice) has been rated by participants, over and over, as *the most valuable part of the training.* It is a tried, tested, and successful method.

Managing the Group Training Session: Tips for Trainers

This section will help trainers get the most out of the experience of leading these activities. Suggestions are included to help trainers prepare for and conduct a successful session, receive feedback on the session from participants, evaluate their skill in delivering the session, and decide what to do differently in subsequent training sessions. Experienced trainers will undoubtedly be able to conduct the activities without reading these suggestions. However, those with less experience can benefit from considering the tips and suggestions provided here.

The exercises in this book are designed to give participants maximum opportunity to interact with one another and contribute to the content and learning of each session. Most of the activities are designed to allow participants' knowledge and experience to become part of the course content. In a few exercises, it will be necessary for you, the trainer, to present concepts and material that will be important to the learning for that session. These should be brief presentations/opening discussions with opportunities for questions to promote understanding. They are meant as foundational material and should not take up a great deal of time. The key to success in conducting all of these activities is to get into the exercises *as quickly as possible* and keep your explanations and presentations to a minimum.

Your primary role is one of *facilitator.* In this capacity you will guide the learning process by giving directions, creating structure, stimulating and leading discussions, recording people's ideas, and generally remaining neutral. Your main responsibilities are to set the tone for the activity, keep the pace moving, observe the small group activities, clarify confusion, lead debriefing sessions, summarize discussions, and create "closure" at the end of the session. It is important to assimilate participants' knowledge and experience into this process.

Assessing Your Readiness to Facilitate the Activities

To facilitate this workshop, you must be an experienced facilitator and trainer. Some activities will be easier to lead than others. Refer to the Overview of Activities, page 8; the "Trainer's Code" indicates the level of training difficulty. It will be up to you to decide whether you have the skills to facilitate each activity, based on the process and material provided. Some groups will require more skill than others to train because of the group dynamics involved and/or the skill level of the participants. If you are relatively new to training, you will gain knowledge and skill by conducting less risky sessions before trying the more difficult ones.

To minimize problems you may have during the training session, make sure you understand the process thoroughly and have all materials handy when conducting the activity. Read through the activity carefully and determine places where something might occur to shift the process and have a "what if" plan in place. If participants start to pull the activity in a different direction than intended, simply stop and refer back to the goals for the activity. Explain that, even though the diversion may be an important one, it is important to keep to the goals and process of the activity at hand.

The attitudes you bring to the workshop will influence the learning of the participants. You will benefit from having a sincere belief in the importance of facilitation and its potential to make groups of people efficient and productive. Some other important attitudes and attributes you will need to conduct successful team leader training are

- Respect for individual differences;
- Belief that the knowledge and experiences of the participants will provide a wealth of information in the learning session;
- Ability to listen actively to all participants and to remain neutral during discussions;
- Willingness to learn from participants; and
- Confidence in the material presented.

Whatever level of experience you have, obtaining feedback from your participants is a key to continually developing your skills as a trainer/facilitator. Suggestions for getting feedback from the participants are included in the "Wrapping Up the Session" section.

Selecting Participants

Mixing experienced with novice team leaders in the training activities enhances the value of discussions and gives experienced leaders the chance to informally mentor less-experienced leaders. It is also important, however, to separate the novice from the experienced team leader in some of the activities; for example, for the most basic activities, novice team leaders can effectively be trained together.

Preparing for the Session

1. Meet with your client and review the needs of those you will be training. Identify the *purpose* of the training.

2. Review the activities and use the information provided in the "How to Use This Book" section to select the appropriate ones. You have the options of (1) conducting activities on an as-needed basis or (2) grouping activities to create a training "program."

3. Carefully review the selected activity to determine whether to adapt it for your client's needs.

4. Gather the necessary materials and read through the suggested resources to familiarize yourself with the content that will be presented/discussed.

5. Prepare any presentation/visual materials or "lecturette" notes you will need for the session.

6. Review the discussion questions included with the exercise. Revise these, if necessary, to ensure that the purpose of the training is accomplished.

7. Read through the entire activity and anticipate any training problems you might encounter. Make a note of your contingency plans.

8. If possible, get together with another trainer (or work with a co-facilitator) and discuss the activity. Focus on opportunities to expand the learning, avoid pitfalls, or deal with difficulties that may come up.

9. Draft the handouts, visuals, and flip charts you will need during the session.

10. Run through the activity in your mind, visualizing how it will go if all goes smoothly. Think of details, such as how handouts will be delivered, where breakout groups will meet, how subgroups will be divided up, what visuals need to be created ahead of time, etc.

11. Revise handouts, visuals, and flip charts, if necessary. Assemble all materials called for and double-check to make sure you have plenty of materials for the size of group you will be training.

12. Set up the room.

Introducing the Session

Welcome everyone to the session and announce the objectives for the activity. Briefly have each person state his or her name and responsibility (or use a quick warm-up activity to get people acquainted with one another). If you use a warm-up activity, add the time it will take to the estimated time for the exercise.

Conducting the Activity

1. Begin the activity with minimal presentation and instruction. If the exercise begins with a group discussion, keep the pace moving. Use the beginning discussions as starters and don't get bogged down.

2. Conduct the activity based on the suggested flow, checking frequently to see if any of the subgroups are confused or are proceeding incorrectly. Otherwise, do not interfere with the work of the subgroups. Remind participants of the rules or time constraints, if necessary. Adapt the rules or time constraints if called for.

3. Bring the exercise to a conclusion.

4. Lead a debriefing discussion as suggested in the activity. The purpose of the post-activity discussion is to clarify and share participants' insights, allow questions, and move toward a summary of important points. Structure the debriefing session to allow participants a chance to report on what they learned from the activity, ask questions, or raise concerns. If appropriate, ask participants to decide actions to be taken or to create checklists or useful material that will be copied and routed to all participants after the session. (See each activity for specific suggestions.)

5. Record useful insights and ideas on flip charts for all to see and organize them so that they can be transcribed and distributed to the participants later, if desired, or as called for in the activity.

6. Remember that the activity is meant to stimulate participants' thinking and creativity, with the end result of increasing everyone's knowledge and/or creating helpful tools to use back on the job. The summarization activities are a critical way to assure that learning has occurred and that closure on the topic has been reached.

Wrapping Up the Session

1. Announce the completion of the activity.

2. Return to the posted objectives and read them aloud to the group. Point out how the stated objectives were accomplished.

3. Be clear about any agreed-on, post-session commitments (e.g., copies of material to be distributed to participants, etc.); be sure to name a person responsible and a deadline.

4. Ask for feedback on the activity and the learning session.

Importance of Receiving Feedback from Participants

At the end of a session is the best time to get feedback, while the activity is fresh in everyone's mind. An effective approach is to allow about five minutes for verbal feedback at the end of each of the activities. Write the word "Helpful" at the top of a flip chart and ask, "What was particularly helpful to you about this session/activity?" Record the responses briefly for all to see. Write the words "More helpful if. . ." at the top of a different flip chart and ask, "What would have made the session/activity better? What could we do differently the next time?" Again, record the responses briefly for all to see.

While listening to the feedback, be sure to write the responses to reflect what was actually said (don't reword them); listen intently and ask for clarification if needed, and *do not respond to the feedback with explanations, defenses, or elaborations*. This type of feedback session is most productive when the trainer simply listens and records. Thank the participants for their feedback. Show genuine appreciation for the comments and explain that these inputs will help you refine successive sessions with them or other participants.

Receiving this type of feedback is invaluable to you as a trainer. First, you will receive positive comments and information that tell you what to continue doing. Second, you will hear simple suggestions you can implement with little effort to improve subsequent sessions. Third, you will have information that may help you make major changes to the activities or to your training in the future.

As you adapt your training, based on participant feedback, several things will happen:

- Your training sessions will be more dynamic and run more smoothly;
- You will feel more confident;
- You will gain insight into the variety of ways people learn;
- You will be able to think more quickly on your feet;
- You will learn to pace your sessions appropriately;
- You will enjoy the process more; and
- The quality of the learning and the training will improve.

Following Up After the Session

As soon as possible after the session, do the following:

1. Debrief with your client. Ask your client for feedback he or she has received from participants. Offer your assessment of how the session went, what its strengths were, and what would have improved the session. Share the participant feedback with the client. Offer any suggestions you may have about upcoming sessions or further training. Thank the client for the opportunity to do the training.

2. Make notes to yourself about the session.

3. Follow up with any commitments you made to the group. It is important that participants receive any material or information promised to them during the session.

4. Note any corrections that need to be made to the materials, if you intend to run the activity again in the future.

Resources

Rees, F. (1998). *The facilitator excellence handbook.* San Francisco: Pfeiffer.

This book explains facilitation skills, techniques, and tools and is a resource to both trainers and facilitative leaders. (*Note:* A second edition of this book is due out in 2005, and the title may change.)

Rees, F. (2001). *How to LEAD work teams: Facilitation skills* (2nd ed.). San Francisco: Pfeiffer.

This book explains the L.E.A.D. model (on which *25 Activities for Developing Team Leaders* is based) and discusses the concepts and skills required for facilitative leadership.

SECTION 1

UNDERSTANDING TEAM LEADERSHIP

EFFECTIVE TEAMWORK can be defined as "people working productively together toward a common goal." If this is the essence of good teamwork, an effective team leader is "one who takes a leadership role in getting people to work productively together."

For a team to function at its optimum, the effective team leader gets people to apply their skills, knowledge, creativity, and expertise in a systematic and efficient way to accomplish the team's goals. The team leader, rather than making all the decisions, doing the work, or making all the plans for the work, draws on the team members to carry out these responsibilities. In this way of working, the team leader takes on the *facilitative leadership* role and directs the *process* of the team's work. The leader gives structure and purpose to the team's work, while allowing team members to make decisions and solve problems in relation to the goals and tasks of the team. As the team matures, the team leader may lead the team to become more and more self-managed, thus giving the team members more control over the process of the team's work.

There are four key concepts facilitative team leaders understand and embrace: (1) teams have common needs, and the team leader must set in place resources and processes to meet those needs; (2) leader behaviors range from controlling to facilitating, and, although leaders must direct and control certain aspects of teamwork, a facilitative style of leadership is highly important when developing high-performing, self-sufficient work teams; (3) the team leader's role is to direct the *process* of teamwork and to lead the team to take responsibility for the *content* (decisions, plans, and followthrough) of the team's work; (4) the leader's role is not a static one, but evolves and fluctuates with the inevitable changes teams face, such as team member turnover, changing team goals, environmental and organizational issues, and the team's development as a team.

Activities in This Section

The activities in this section will help team leaders develop a conceptual foundation for becoming facilitative team leaders. They are based on the L.E.A.D. model of leadership in which facilitative leadership is at the core. Activity 1 uses a Leadership Style Questionnaire to help team leaders relate their own behaviors to three styles of leadership: controlling, collaborative, or facilitative. This sets the tone for many of the activities in the book and is highly recommended as part of any team leader training. The other activities focus on the L.E.A.D. model and basic principles of effective team leadership.

Activity 1, Leadership Style Questionnaire, is designed to start team leaders thinking about behaviors and practices that link to leadership styles. Three leadership styles are identified and discussed: controlling, collaborative, and facilitative. After taking the questionnaire, team leaders discuss the results of their self-ratings and discuss the advantages and disadvantages of each style, noting examples of when it is appropriate to use each style.

Activity 2, L.E.A.D. Bingo, adapts the game of Bingo to quiz participants on the components and concepts of the L.E.A.D. model. The goal of the exercise is to give participants a foundational knowledge of the L.E.A.D. model.

Activity 3, Teamwork Step-by-Step, introduces participants to a ten-step process for developing and leading a team, from inception through the disbanding or restructuring of the team. Participants work in subgroups of three to four people each to answer a list of questions about the steps they have been assigned. Subgroups present their answers to the large group, and a general discussion follows. The purpose of this activity is to get team leaders to look at the big picture of team leadership and to think about how to approach teamwork in a step-by-step manner. The activity emphasizes the importance of working with two important dimensions of teamwork: (1) to bring the team along in its development as a team, and (2) to lead it through the formulation and *achievement* of its goals.

Activity 4, What Teams Need, focuses team leaders on what teams need in order to function well. Participants are given ten key needs of teams and are asked to present and discuss them for review. Once the meaning of each of the needs is discussed, participants will prioritize the list, decide which of the ten items are most neglected in teams, and make suggestions as to how team leaders can use this information to build stronger teams.

Activity 5, Leadership Values Auction, gives team leaders a chance to reflect on important team leader values in two distinctly different leadership situations. Through the process of two auctions, participants bid on values they consider most important in the two different situations. Each auction is discussed, giving participants a chance to understand both their own and others' reasons for bidding on certain values.

Below is a brief overview of the L.E.A.D. model. For further discussion and supporting material, refer to *How to LEAD Work Teams: Facilitation Skills* (2nd ed.), San Francisco: Pfeiffer, 2001.

The L.E.A.D. Model

L—Lead with a Clear Purpose.   To lead with a clear purpose simply means to use goals as a motivator for teams. For goals to motivate people, they must be challenging, positive, and realistic. The team must have its own goals that support the larger organization's goals. Some ways the team leader can ensure that the team has clear purpose are to lead the team in defining its mission, stating and publishing its goals, tracking progress toward those goals, revising the goals as needed, and holding results-oriented team meetings that propel the team toward completing its goals.

E—Empower to Participate.   The word "empower" means to give power or authority, to authorize, to enable or permit. Even when the team members are motivated by the team's goals, they become unmotivated if they cannot participate in important decisions regarding how the team achieves those goals, especially if they are expected to carry out those decisions. A facilitative team leader can *facilitate team members* to set the team's goals, lay out plans to achieve those goals, make important decisions along the way, assign roles and responsibilities, solve problems, and evaluate the progress of the team.

A—Aim for Consensus.   A key role of the team leader is to guide the team in the process of reaching general agreement (consensus) on important decisions. Even when all members do not agree that a particular decision is the best way to go, the team leader can receive commitment from all members to support the decision 100 percent. Effective team leaders prefer their teams to reach consensus using a balanced and open process, since decisions reached in this manner generally receive a higher level of support than do decisions made without consensus.

D—Direct the Process.   To successfully direct the process of teamwork requires experience in working with groups and knowledge about the group process. An effective team leader will use various techniques to make sure the team accomplishes its tasks and that people work together in a congenial and supportive way. A facilitative team leader will let team members decide much about the *content* of their work, but will give the team clear structure in the *process* of how the team works together. For example, a facilitative team leader will draw out team members' ideas and let them make a decision on how the team will proceed on a particular project. At the same time, the team leader will be firm about the structure (*process*) of the meeting during which that decision is made, ensuring that all members' ideas are included and that an effective consensus method is used. To "direct the process" does not mean to order the team about in a directive manner; it means to guide the team by suggesting ways to structure its work so that team members, the team as a whole, and the organization benefit as much as possible.

Leadership Style Questionnaire

Purpose

- To understand the differences between controlling, collaborative, and facilitative leadership behaviors
- To identify individual leadership preferences and their impact on teams
- To identify opportunities to improve team leader effectiveness

Time

1 1/2 hours

Group Size

Designed for twelve to eighteen people

Materials

- Flip chart and marking pens for the facilitator
- Pencil for each participant
- One copy of the Leadership Style Questionnaire for each participant
- One copy of the Scoring the Leadership Style Questionnaire for each participant
- One copy of the Response to the Leadership Style Questionnaire for each participant

Room Setup

U-shape: set tables in a "U" with chairs around the outside of the "U" so all participants can see one another. Place the flip chart in the open space at the top of the "U," as shown in the diagram:

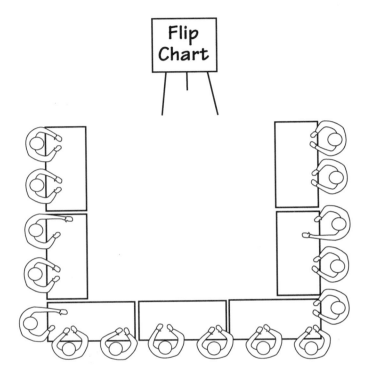

Steps

1. *Introduce the session.* Explain the purpose of the session: (1) to get team leaders to think about the behaviors and approaches they use in relation to leading a team and (2) to discuss what modification of these behaviors will help them be more effective team leaders.

2. *Explain the process.* Ask the team leaders to answer each item as honestly as possible, based on the way they typically behave as team leaders. Assure them that the scores will be for their use only and that they will be free to discuss with others whatever they choose about their scores or answers. Distribute the Leadership Style Questionnaire and pencils, and give directions for completing it.

3. *Complete the questionnaire.* Ask each team leader to take and score the questionnaire. Once everyone has completed the questionnaire,

hand out copies of the Scoring the Leadership Style Questionnaire sheet and allow them to score their own questionnaires. Briefly go over what the scores indicate, based on the "Interpreting Your Score" section at the end of the scoring sheet.

4. *Discuss the results.* The purpose of this part of the exercise is to give team leaders the opportunity (1) to express their ideas in relation to their own leadership style and (2) to practice effective listening while another person speaks. Divide the group into pairs. Distribute a copy of the Response to the Leadership Style Questionnaire to each participant. Each person will complete each statement on the Response to the Leadership Style Questionnaire, while the other person listens. The speaker should be as *honest* as possible when speaking, and the listener should try to listen *intently* when the other person talks. The listener should not give advice or bring up his or her own personal anecdotes while the speaker is relating his or her ideas. The listener may ask a few questions, if necessary, to learn more (to probe) or to clarify what the speaker is saying. Listeners, however, should minimize their "talk." After each speaker has completed the statements, the listener responds briefly to show he or she has heard and related to what the speaker said. Then the partners switch roles. The process is

   • Speaker answers all the questions. Listener listens.

   • Listener responds briefly to acknowledge or clarify speaker's comments.

   • Partners switch roles.

5. *Discuss the concepts.* Bring the group back together and give a short lecture on the meaning of the three styles: controlling, collaborative, and facilitative. (Refer to *How to Lead Work Teams: Facilitation Skills,* Chapter 4, "From Controlling to Facilitating" for a discussion of these leadership styles.) Ask the following discussion questions, while noting key learning points on a flip chart for all to see.

   • What are some advantages and disadvantages of each style?

   • Give an example of a situation in which it would be appropriate to use a "controlling" style. In what situations would a "controlling" style hinder the team's success?

   • Give an example of a situation in which it would be appropriate to use a "collaborative" style. In what situations would a "collaborative" style hinder the team's success?

- Give an example of a situation in which it would be appropriate to use a "facilitative" style. In what situations would a "facilitative" style hinder the team's success?

6. *Conclude the session.* Close the session by asking the group to highlight two or three key learnings from the activity and discussion. Read the objectives for the session and point out that the group accomplished the purpose of the session. If desired, ask for feedback on the session (See "Managing the Group Training Session" in the Introduction) and adjourn the group.

About the Leadership Style Questionnaire

The Leadership Style Questionnaire is not a statistically validated survey/questionnaire. It represents behaviors that are generally linked to the three styles of leadership: controlling, collaborative, and facilitative. It was designed as a learning tool and a framework for discussion and is intended to allow team leaders an opportunity to:

- Think about their own leadership *behaviors* in relation to three identified styles;

- Discuss leadership styles and behaviors with others; and

- Consider why and how they might adapt their own leadership style to better accommodate teams.

LEADERSHIP STYLE QUESTIONNAIRE

Instructions: Respond to the statements below as honestly as possible. Consider how you act in *most situations* as a team leader. Circle the *letter* of the response that best describes your behavior.

1. When discussing a difficult issue with people on my team, I most often:

    a. Express my opinions and offer a solution.

    b. Listen first to the opinions of others and suggest a mutual solution.

    c. Ask for people's opinions and summarize what I heard.

2. If team members are not attending team meetings, I:

    a. Call everyone together (with suitable reward and motivation for attending) and ask team members what needs to happen to get better attendance at team meetings.

    b. Go to each team member and ask each one what will improve team meeting attendance, then decide what to do.

    c. Send a notice to all team members stating that meeting attendance is mandatory.

3. At a meeting of my team, I am most comfortable when:

    a. Listening, asking questions, and recording group inputs.

    b. Presenting and/or having others present.

    c. Letting someone else facilitate while I participate as a team member.

4. To make sure my team is pursuing the right goals, I am most apt to:

    a. Collaborate with the team to determine what the team's goals should be.

    b. Review upper management's expectations with the team and then have the team define its specific goals.

    c. Tell the team what its goals are, based on input I get from upper management.

5. When leading a team meeting, I always:

    a. Have someone take meeting notes to distribute after the meeting.

    b. Use flip charts or white boards to record team member inputs and decisions.

    c. Wait until the end of the meeting and write down only the decisions and action items.

6. When I take on the role of neutral facilitator, I:

    a. Enjoy remaining neutral while others come up with ideas.

    b. Want very badly to chime in with my opinions and solutions.

    c. Am comfortable occasionally giving input to the discussion and then quickly returning to the role of neutral facilitator.

7. When participating in a group meeting, I am:

    a. Strong and outspoken in my opinions.

    b. Skilled at getting both my own and others' opinions considered.

    c. Skilled at drawing out the ideas of others to open new doors for creativity and problem solving.

8. When leading a group meeting, I:

    a. Don't know how to summarize a group discussion.

    b. Am comfortable summarizing what the group has said.

    c. Summarize group inputs to work to my advantage.

9. When the synergy of my team leads it to a conclusion I do not support, I:

    a. Tell the group I cannot support the decision.

    b. Ask the group to rethink its conclusion based on evidence I cite.

    c. Support the group's decision even when I don't agree 100 percent.

10. When leading a team meeting, if the energy level and urgency move in a direction other than the agenda, I:

    a. Invite the group to suggest alterations.

    b. Alter the agenda to fit the needs of the group.

    c. Stick to the agenda.

11. When leading a team, I am most apt to:

    a. Present some guidelines for appropriate team behavior and ask team members to add some of their own.

    b. Facilitate the team to set its own guidelines for appropriate team behavior.

    c. Set and publish guidelines for appropriate team behavior.

12. When I am the expert on a subject the team is dealing with, I:

    a. Wear two hats while facilitating the meeting: remaining neutral when possible and contributing when needed.

    b. Let someone else facilitate the meeting while I act as a team member.

    c. Influence the team with my advice and approach, while leading the team meeting.

SCORING THE LEADERSHIP STYLE QUESTIONNAIRE

Instructions: Give yourself a point score by tallying up the points related to each of your responses. Use the points designated below.

Question 1:   a = 1   b = 2   c = 3   Your points for Question 1: _____

Question 2:   a = 3   b = 2   c = 1   Your points for Question 2: _____

Question 3:   a = 3   b = 1   c = 2   Your points for Question 3: _____

Question 4:   a = 2   b = 3   c = 1   Your points for Question 4: _____

Question 5:   a = 1   b = 3   c = 2   Your points for Question 5: _____

Question 6:   a = 3   b = 1   c = 2   Your points for Question 6: _____

Question 7:   a = 1   b = 2   c = 3   Your points for Question 7: _____

Question 8:   a = 2   b = 3   c = 1   Your points for Question 8: _____

Question 9:   a = 1   b = 2   c = 3   Your points for Question 9: _____

Question 10:   a = 3   b = 2   c = 1   Your points for Question 10: _____

Question 11:   a = 2   b = 3   c = 1   Your points for Question 11: _____

Question 12:   a = 2   b = 3   c = 1   Your points for Question 12: _____

POINT TOTAL: _____

INTERPRETING YOUR SCORE

If you scored in the *low range,* 12 to 18 points, you lean toward being a controlling team leader. You can undoubtedly benefit by becoming more collaborative and facilitative in your approach to team leadership. There are many times when it will benefit you and your organization to actively solicit and incorporate the ideas of others in your decisions. There are times when the best approach will be to guide others to come up with the best solution. Gaining skill and practice in facilitation will broaden and enhance your leadership skills, giving you more opportunities to be an effective leader.

If you scored in the *medium range,* 19 to 30 points, you are definitely a collaborative team leader and somewhat comfortable with facilitating. You tend to work with others by contributing your ideas as well as encouraging others to contribute theirs. You work toward agreement by trying to incorporate both your own and others' ideas. There are times when a good leader should remain neutral and facilitate others' coming up with a solution. Improving your fundamental facilitation skills and getting more practice as a facilitator will help you expand and refine your facilitative leadership skills.

If you scored in the *high range,* 31 to 36 points, you are a highly facilitative leader and quite comfortable with facilitating. This is your preferred way to lead. You are effective at drawing others out and getting them to come to a decision. You are likely to be a sought-after team leader. Remember, however, that the facilitation approach, although powerful and effective, should not be used to the exclusion of other methods. There may be times when your team will need you to be more directive or involved in the content of a decision, for example:

- When you are the technical/professional "expert" in relation to the decision;
- When you will play a critical role in implementing the decision;
- When you must interpret the boundaries or constraints that the organization will place on the decision.

No matter how you scored, remember there are times when facilitation is by far the best approach and times when another approach is called for.

RESPONSE TO THE LEADERSHIP STYLE QUESTIONNAIRE

When speaking with your partner, complete the following statements as honestly as possible:

1. My initial response to the results of this questionnaire is . . .

2. Based on this questionnaire, my preferred style of leadership is . . .

3. Some examples of how I lead using this style are . . .

4. I am uncomfortable using the . . . style of leadership because . . .

5. My leadership strengths are . . .

6. I could improve my leadership style by doing more . . . and by doing less . . .

7. In my organization, there are . . . (select one response below and explain).
   a. Sufficient incentives to be a facilitative leader.
   b. Obstacles to being a facilitative leader.
   c. Both (explain).

ACTIVITY 2

L.E.A.D. Bingo*

Purpose

- To understand the four components of the L.E.A.D. Model of leadership
- To participate in a Bingo game and team competition
- To identify L.E.A.D. Model concepts and apply these to team leader behaviors and practices

Time

1 hour

Group Size

Designed for twelve to twenty people, three to five teams of four or five people each

Materials

- Flip chart and marking pen for the facilitator
- Pen/pencil for each participant
- One L.E.A.D. Model Bingo Card for each person
- One L.E.A.D. Model Bingo Questions and Answers Sheet for the instructor
- One L.E.A.D. Model handout per participant

*Adapted from Team Bingo, in *Teamwork and Teamplay* by S. Thiagarajan and G. Parker, 1999, San Francisco: Pfeiffer.

Room Setup

An arrangement of chairs and tables (optional) that allows for up to five teams of four to five people each to sit in teams and to see the rest of the group and the facilitator.

Steps

1. *Introduce the session.* Explain the purpose of the activity and emphasize that it is designed to be a fun way to reinforce concepts of leadership based on the L.E.A.D. Model. (If possible, before the session, ask participants to read Chapter 3 of *How to Lead Work Teams.*) Alternatively, give a brief lecturette on the highlights of the model. If you prepare any handouts, do not distribute them until the end of the session.

2. *Announce the rules.* Divide the group into teams of four to five people each. Read the following rules aloud:

   A definition will be read aloud. Once the definition has been completely read, the first person to stand up will be allowed to answer the question. A "referee" will be appointed to announce who the first person was each time. If the first person standing selects the correct term or phrase, his or her team will be allowed to place an "X" through the box containing that answer. If the answer is incorrect, the team will be required to eliminate an "X" already on its cards or, if the team has no Xs, it will not be allowed to participate in the next round. If the answer is incorrect, another team will be allowed to answer the question, and so on. When a team gets Xs in all boxes in one row or column, or diagonally across the whole card, it should call out "Bingo."

3. *Conduct the game.* Distribute a L.E.A.D. Model Bingo Card and a pen or pencil to each person. Read the items one at a time from the L.E.A.D. Model Bingo Questions and Answers Sheet. When the first person standing (as determined by the referee, if necessary) says his or her answer, state either "correct" or "incorrect." Based on the rules you read, allow a second team to answer if someone is standing. If the answer is incorrect after the third try, go on to the next item and come back to this one at the end. Keep reading the definitions until all have been covered or if a team gets Bingo. If a team gets Bingo, read through the remaining items to determine the second-place winner.

4. *Conclude the session.* Debrief the session by asking if anyone needs clarification on any of the items. Ask if anyone has questions about the L.E.A.D. Model. If so, discuss them. For feedback, ask how participants would change the game to increase what they learned. As a takeaway, give everyone a copy of The L.E.A.D. Model handout.

Variation

Consider giving small prizes to the winning team or all teams that get Bingo before all questions are read. Prizes should be something that all team members can share, such as a box of candy, pens, etc.

Resource

Rees, F. (2001). *How to LEAD Work Teams: Facilitation Skills* (2nd ed.). San Francisco: Pfeiffer.

L.E.A.D. MODEL BINGO CARD

Lead with a Clear Purpose	Facilitator	Listening, Asking Questions, and Recording Ideas	Telling, Selling, and Directing	Empower to Participate
Participative Team Meeting	Discourage Participation	Direct the Process	Support Those Decisions	Positive Force to Be Shared for Good of All
Ownership and Buy-In	Active Listening	Facilitative Leader	Maximize Team Member Participation	To Empower
Keep the Team on Track	Self-Sufficient Team	Open-Ended Questions	Reach Consensus	Less Committed and Less Responsible
Working Collaboratively	Controlling Leadership Style	Record Ideas for All to See	Personal Agendas	Neutral

L.E.A.D. MODEL BINGO
QUESTIONS AND ANSWERS SHEET

1. A team leader who frequently involves the team in solving problems and making decisions. (*Answer:* Facilitative leader)

2. When a team leader makes sure all members of the team know what the overall team goals and boundaries are, he or she is carrying out which arm of the L.E.A.D. Model? (*Answer:* Lead with a clear purpose)

3. Leaders who take credit for their teams' efforts to make decisions must then. . . . (*Answer:* Discourage participation)

4. When a team leader directs the decisions and work of the team without any team member input, he or she is acting in what manner? (*Answer:* Controlling leadership style)

5. To give power or authority, to authorize, to enable or permit means . . . . (*Answer:* To empower)

6. A team meeting in which all team members are contributing ideas, developing solutions, and working together to reach consensus can be called a . . . . (*Answer:* Participative team meeting)

7. When team members feel over-controlled by the team leader, they will probably be . . . . (*Answer:* Less committed and less responsible)

8. When team members are mainly committed to their own individual goals, what is taking precedence over the team's goals? (*Answer:* Personal agendas)

9. A technique that draws out responses and ideas from team members. (*Answer:* Open-ended questions)

10. A person responsible for guiding and structuring the process of a team meeting without expressing opinions on the content of the meeting. (*Answer:* Facilitator)

11. When the team leader and team members all work together to solve a problem, find a solution, or deal with the day-to-day work of the team, it is said that they are . . . . (*Answer:* Working collaboratively)

12. When a team leader takes responsibility for overseeing how teamwork is progressing and makes suggestions to the team accordingly, he or she is carrying out which arm of the L.E.A.D. Model? (*Answer:* Direct the process)

13. To work through differences of opinions, disagreements, and conflict to reach a solution that everyone can support 100 percent. (*Answer:* Reach consensus)

14. When a team leader makes an effort to hear and understand all ideas or points made by a team member before interrupting, he or she is demonstrating what behavior? (*Answer:* Active listening)

15. When team leaders strive to have team members working *with* rather than *for* them, what arm of the L.E.A.D. Model are they carrying out? (*Answer:* Empower to participate)

16. When facilitating, it is best for a team leader to remain . . . . (*Answer:* Neutral)

25 Activities for Developing Team Leaders. Copyright © 2005 by John Wiley & Sons, Inc. Reproduced by permission of Pfeiffer, an Imprint of Wiley. www.pfeiffer.com

17. A controlling leader's behaviors include: (*Answer:* Telling, selling, and directing)

18. When team members are involved in making and carrying out a decision, it is said they have . . . . (*Answer:* Ownership and buy-in)

19. Instead of viewing power as limited, a facilitative leader views power as a . . . . (*Answer:* Positive force to be shared for good of all)

20. One way a team leader can make sure all ideas are heard and considered is to . . . . (*Answer:* Record ideas for all to see)

21. The techniques of asking questions, listening, summarizing, drawing out different opinions, and recording ideas are intended to . . . . (*Answer:* Maximize team member participation)

22. A facilitative leader's behaviors include: (*Answer:* Listening, asking questions, and recording ideas)

23. An aspect of directing the process of teamwork. (*Answer:* Keep the team on track)

24. An important role of a facilitative team leader is to help the team develop into a . . . . (*Answer:* Self-sufficient team)

25. When a team leader encourages a team to make decisions, it is important that the team leader . . . . (*Answer:* Support those decisions)

THE L.E.A.D. MODEL

L—Lead with a Clear Purpose.   To lead with a clear purpose simply means to use goals as a motivator for teams. For goals to motivate people, they need to be challenging, positive, and realistic. The team must have its own goals that support the larger company goals. Some ways the team leader can ensure that the team has a clear purpose are to lead the team in defining its mission, stating and publishing its goals, tracking progress toward those goals, revising the goals as needed, and holding results-oriented team meetings that propel the team toward completing its goals.

E—Empower to Participate.   The word "empower" means to give power or authority, to authorize, to enable or permit. Even when the team members are motivated by the team's goals, they become unmotivated if they cannot participate in important decisions regarding how the team achieves those goals, especially if they are expected to carry out those decisions. A facilitative team leader can *facilitate team members* to set the team's goals, lay out plans to achieve those goals, make important decisions along the way, assign roles and responsibilities, solve problems, and evaluate the progress of the team.

A—Aim for Consensus.   A key role of the team leader is to guide the team in the process of reaching general agreement (consensus) on important decisions. Even when all members do not agree that a particular decision is the best way to go, the team leader can receive commitment from all members to support the decision 100 percent. Effective team leaders prefer their teams to reach consensus using a balanced and open process, since decisions reached in this manner generally receive a higher level of support than do decisions made without consensus.

D—Direct the Process.   To successfully direct the process of teamwork requires experience in working with groups and knowledge about the group process. An effective team leader will use various techniques to make sure the team accomplishes its tasks and that people work together in a congenial and supportive way. A facilitative team leader will let team members decide much about the *content* of their work, but will give the team clear structure in the *process* of how the team works together. For example, a facilitative team leader will draw out team members' ideas and let them make a decision on how the team will proceed on a particular project. At the same time, the team leader will be firm about the structure (*process*) of the meeting during which that decision is made, ensuring that all members' ideas are included and that an effective consensus method is used. To "direct the process" does not mean to order the team about in a directive manner; it means to guide the team by suggesting ways to structure its work so that team members, the team as a whole, and the organization benefit as much as possible.

Teamwork Step-by-Step*

Purpose

- To explore ten steps in leading and developing a team
- To describe and discuss each step in relation to the role and responsibilities of a team leader
- To identify the challenges each step poses and discuss potential ways of overcoming these challenges

Time

2 to 2 1/2 hours

Group Size

Designed for fifteen to twenty people; five subgroups of three to four participants each

Materials

- A copy of the 10 Steps to Effective Teamwork flow chart for each participant

*Note: Familiarize yourself with the ten steps in teamwork as presented in *Teamwork from Start to Finish: Ten Steps to Results* (Rees, 1997) so you can correct misconceptions and enhance the learning from this activity. You should be clear about the purpose and reason for each step, as well as the process to achieve it. (See Resource section at the end of this activity.)

- A pencil and clipboard (or other portable writing surface) for each participant
- A copy of the 10 Steps Questions to Answer handout for each participant
- A flip chart, markers, and masking tape for each subgroup
- A flip chart, markers, and masking tape for the instructor
- Two or three flip charts, prepared ahead of time and posted on the wall, showing the 10 Steps to Effective Teamwork flow chart (identical to the handout)
- A flip chart prepared ahead of time with the following written on it:

  Role of a Team Leader: (1) To bring the team along in its development as a team, and (2) To lead it in the formulation and achievement of its goals

Room Setup

A room large enough so that five subgroups can gather and complete the assignments without disturbing one another. Movable chairs and plenty of wall space (for posting flip charts) are necessary.

Steps

1. *Announce the goals of the session and introduce the activity.* Explain that the purpose of this activity is to think about the "big picture" of what is involved in forming and leading a team. State that most people agree the main functions of a team leader are (1) to bring the team along in its development as a team, and (2) to lead it in the formulation and achievement of its goals. (Refer to the prepared, posted flip chart.)

   Next, explain that some team experts have identified important things that must happen, or steps that need to be taken, for a team to function well as a team. One author has outlined ten steps that will help a team both develop as a team and achieve its team goals. Refer to the prepared and posted flip charts showing the 10 Steps to Effective Teamwork and explain that in this session, participants are going to look at these ten steps and discuss them in subgroups.

   Read over the ten steps (just the title for each step). Explain that during this session participants will make an effort to understand each step and identify the team leader challenges associated with it. Participants will also be given the chance to delete, change, or add to these steps. Emphasize that the *purpose* of this activity is to *get a big picture of what a team faces,* not to come up with a perfect list of steps. If participants want to discuss or debate the steps at this time, stop them and tell them that they will be discussing the purpose and merits of each step in subgroups and will be given a chance later to make changes to the steps.

2. *Assign subgroups and roles.* Distribute the 10 Steps to Effective Teamwork and the Questions to Answer handouts. Explain that the group will be divided into five subgroups (of three to four members each). Each subgroup will be working on *two* of the 10 Steps to Effective Teamwork. Each subgroup will address the same questions for each of the steps it is reviewing and, later, present their ideas back to the whole group.

3. *Divide the group into five subgroups of three to four participants each,* or as equal distribution of members as possible. Assign two of the ten steps to each subgroup. Assign each subgroup a letter (A, B, C, etc.) and write these letters on a flip chart. Beside each letter indicate the steps that subgroup will work on. The following is a suggested distribution:

   Group A: Steps 1 and 2

   Group B: Steps 3 and 4

   Group C: Steps 5 and 6

   Group D: Steps 7 and 8

   Group E: Steps 9 and 10

Give each subgroup a flip chart, a marking pen, and a roll of masking tape. Instruct each subgroup to follow the directions on the 10 Steps Questions to Answer handout. Tell them to allow 20 to 25 minutes to answer the questions and plan a brief presentation for each step. They will be working in subgroups for about 50 minutes.

While the subgroups are working, go around to each subgroup to see if they are following the directions, or if they have any questions. After 20 to 25 minutes, tell the subgroups they should be wrapping up the discussion of the first step and moving on to the next. After about 45 minutes, remind the subgroups that their time is almost up and that they should have a brief presentation on each of the steps. Suggest that they select two different presenters, one to present each step.

4. *Reconvene the large group.* Bring the subgroups back into the large group. Ask subgroups to make their presentations, working through each of the ten steps in order. After each subgroup has presented a

step, ask the rest of the group if anyone has comments or questions for the subgroup presenting. Try to keep the pace moving along. Remind subgroups to keep their presentations brief.

5. *Lead a concluding discussion.* Once all presentations are made, lead a discussion using some or all of the following questions:

   • Do these ten steps adequately cover both dimensions of teamwork: (1) bringing the team along in its *development* as a team, and (2) leading it in the formulation and *achievement* of its goals? Why or why not?

   • What would you do in relation to the ten steps if you were a *new* team leader to a team already in progress?

   • Are there any steps you would delete? Combine? Add? Why?

   • In the "real world" of teams, which of these steps are the most difficult to implement? Why?

   When leading this discussion, be open to suggestions about adding or deleting steps. Just because the ten steps have been outlined doesn't mean they cannot be changed or presented in a different way. Avoid debating the merits of a participant's idea. Write the idea on a flip chart, make sure the idea is understood, and ask what reactions others have to the suggestion.

6. *Wrap up the session.* Go around the room and ask each person to answer this question: *What are some of the more valuable ideas or techniques you have heard about today that will help you as a team leader?*

   Review the purpose of the learning activity, ask for feedback on the exercise (see "Managing the Group Training Session: Tips for Trainers" in the Introduction) and adjourn.

Variation

To shorten the activity, give a brief presentation of the ten steps. Then divide the group into subgroups and have each subgroup answer only questions 4, 5, and 6. Bring the subgroups back together to discuss the challenges and ways to overcome them.

Resource

Rees, F. (1997). *Teamwork from Start to Finish: Ten Steps to Results.* San Francisco: Pfeiffer.

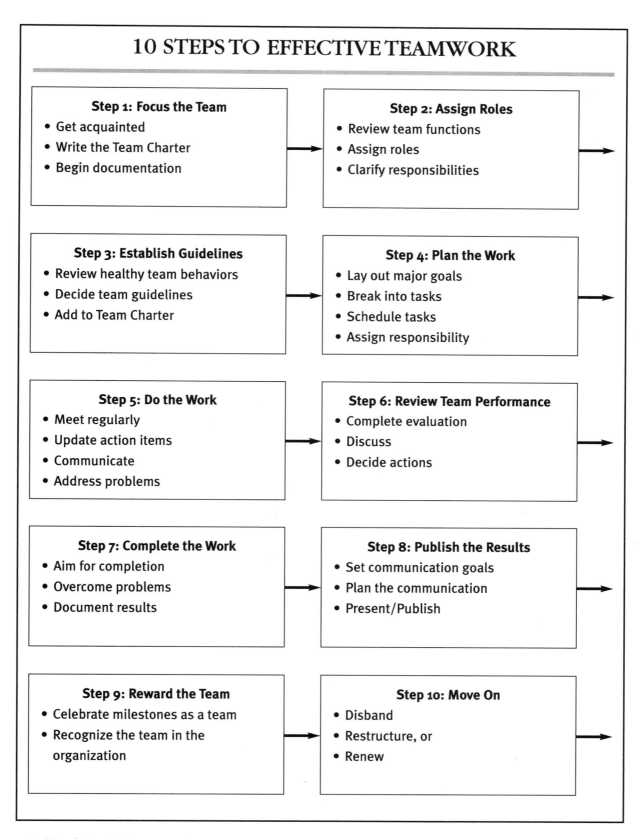

10 STEPS TO EFFECTIVE TEAMWORK

Step 1: Focus the Team
- Get acquainted
- Write the Team Charter
- Begin documentation

Step 2: Assign Roles
- Review team functions
- Assign roles
- Clarify responsibilities

Step 3: Establish Guidelines
- Review healthy team behaviors
- Decide team guidelines
- Add to Team Charter

Step 4: Plan the Work
- Lay out major goals
- Break into tasks
- Schedule tasks
- Assign responsibility

Step 5: Do the Work
- Meet regularly
- Update action items
- Communicate
- Address problems

Step 6: Review Team Performance
- Complete evaluation
- Discuss
- Decide actions

Step 7: Complete the Work
- Aim for completion
- Overcome problems
- Document results

Step 8: Publish the Results
- Set communication goals
- Plan the communication
- Present/Publish

Step 9: Reward the Team
- Celebrate milestones as a team
- Recognize the team in the organization

Step 10: Move On
- Disband
- Restructure, or
- Renew

10 STEPS QUESTIONS TO ANSWER

Instructions: Appoint a facilitator for your subgroup. (Because the subgroups are small, the facilitator may also contribute to the discussion.) Answer all of the questions below for each step you have been assigned. Prepare a *brief* presentation as described below.

To manage your time, spend 15 to 20 minutes discussing each question. Spend another 5 minutes preparing your presentation. After 20 to 25 minutes, move on to the next step.

STEP # _____

1. What is the purpose of this step?

2. Why is it important?

3. What activities are likely to take place during this step?

4. Do you think this step is in the right sequence as presented in the 10 Steps to Effective Teamwork? Why or why not?

5. What are some challenges a team leader may face in getting the team to accomplish this step?

6. What are some ways a team leader can overcome these challenges?

Once you have answered the questions for each step, prepare a *brief* presentation using a prepared flip chart, and select someone from your subgroup to *present the following* back to the large group:

- Your answers to Questions 1, 2, and 3.
- One or two challenges a team leader might face during this step.
- One or two suggestions to help a team leader overcome these challenges.

STEP # _____

1. What is the purpose of this step?

2. Why is it important?

3. What activities are likely to take place during this step?

4. What are some challenges a team leader may face in getting the team to accomplish this step?

5. Has any team you have led or been on run into challenges when accomplishing this step? What happened? How were these challenges met?

6. What are some ways a team leader can overcome these challenges?

Once you have answered the questions for each step, prepare a brief presentation using a prepared flip chart, and select someone from your subgroup to *present the following* back to the large group:

- Your answers to Questions #1, 2, and 3.
- One or two challenges a team leader might face during this step.
- One or two suggestions to help a team leader overcome these challenges.

What Teams Need

Goals

- To identify and discuss ten important needs of teams
- To identify the three most important needs
- To select the three or four most often neglected of these needs in today's teams and discuss actions team leaders can take to ensure that team needs are met

Time

2 to 2 1/2 hours

Group Size

Sixteen to twenty people, divided into subgroups of four or five members each

Materials

- Flip chart and marking pens for each subgroup and for the facilitator
- Pen/pencil and paper for each participant
- One set of 3 x 5 cards with one of the ten key needs printed on each card from the What Teams Need handout
- Six blank 3 x 5 cards for each participant

- Two flip charts, each with a copy of the What Teams Need diagram (one to indicate the most important needs (labeled "Most Important Needs") and one to indicate the three or four most neglected needs (labeled "Most Neglected Needs")
- One copy per participant of the What Teams Need diagram

Room Setup

Round tables with room for five people per table, placed in the room so that everyone can see the front of the room when necessary. If round tables are not available, use a large U-shape setup and group the subgroups in different sections, with chairs placed both inside and outside the "U." Each subgroup should have a flip chart and markers.

Steps

1. *Introduce the session.* Explain the purpose of the session: to discuss important needs of teams and how team leaders can support these needs. Divide the group into subgroups of four to five people each, with each subgroup seated at a round table near a flip chart. Hand out paper and pens or pencils.

2. *Hold small group discussions.* Distribute the 3 x 5 cards among the tables as evenly as possible and instruct the participants at each table to do the following: (1) discuss the meaning of each card (need); (2) discuss why this is a key need; (3) discuss how one can determine that this need is being met on a team; and (4) name one or two team leader actions that support this need. Each subgroup should list its key points on a flip chart.

3. *Large group discussion.* After 30 to 45 minutes, reconvene the large group and distribute one copy per person of the What Teams Need diagram and show the diagram using a flip chart. For each of the ten needs, ask the subgroup that worked on that need to report on the four assignments above. Once the reporting team is finished, ask the rest of the group if anyone has any comments or questions relating to that item. Go through all the items until all the meanings and examples have been discussed. Try to reach the point where there is general agreement as to the meaning of each item.

4. *Label the list.* Explain that for the rest of the session, participants are going to do three things: (1) prioritize the list; (2) decide which of the ten items are most neglected in teams; and (3) make suggestions as to how team leaders can use this information to build stronger teams. Label each of the items on the list with a letter of the alphabet (A through J). Write the letter beside each item on the flip chart so all can see.

5. *Prioritize the list.* Distribute three blank 3 x 5 cards to each person and ask each person to think about what needs are the most important in teams today. Ask them to select their three top (most important) needs and write the letter of each need on a 3 x 5 card. Allow some time for individuals to think and to complete this task. Next, ask each participant to prioritize their three cards as follows: (1) select the most important item and write the number 3 on the card below the item and circle the number; (2) select the next most important item and write the number 2 on the card below the item and circle the number; and (3) select the next most important item and write the number 1 on the card below the item and circle the number. (Show an example on a flip chart sheet of how the labeled and numbered cards might look.) Collect the completed cards and set them aside. Give the next set of directions before tallying the results.

6. *Determine the most neglected needs.* Distribute three more blank 3 x 5 cards to each person. This time, have participants work *in pairs* to come up with the three *most often neglected needs* in teams today. Encourage pairs to think of their own recent team experiences, preferably as team *members*. Ask them to select their three top (most neglected) needs and write the letter of each need on a 3 x 5 card. Next, ask each pair to prioritize its three items/cards as follows: (1) select the most important neglected item and write the number 3 on the card below the item and circle the number; (2) select the next most important neglected item and write the number 2 on the card below the item and circle the number; and (3) select the next most important neglected item and write the number 1 on the card below the item and circle the number. Each pair will prepare and submit *one* set of 3 x 5 cards with its prioritized neglected needs as described above. (Show an example on a flip chart to show three cards labeled and numbered.) While the pairs are completing this task, tally the first set of 3 x 5 cards and post the results on the flip chart beside the ten items. *Turn the flip chart around so the pairs cannot see the results while working on the second set of cards.*

7. *Discuss the prioritized list.* Show the participants the results of the first prioritized list: the most important of the needs. Lead a discussion using the following questions as a guide:

   - What is your reaction to these results?

   - What surprised you?

   - What confirms what you already knew?

8. *Tally the scores for the most often neglected needs.* Tally the second set of cards by going around the room and asking each pair to submit their items and "scores" for each. Using the second prepared What Teams Need flip chart, write the scores beside each item as you go around the room. Total the scores and select the top three or four items to indicate which needs are most often neglected in teams today, based on the participants' responses. Post this flip chart near the first flip chart showing the prioritization of needs.

9. *Discuss the neglected needs.* Lead a discussion using the following questions as a guide:

   - Why do you think these particular items came out on top as the most neglected in teams today?

   - What differences would it make in teams if these needs were met?

   - What challenges do team leaders face as a result of these needs being neglected?

   - What actions can team leaders take to ensure that these needs are met?

10. *Conclude the session.* Summarize the group's inputs and reinforce the concepts that (1) there are several critical needs that teams have in order to function well and (2) the team leader plays the role of helping team members and the team meet these needs. Ask the team leaders for ideas as to how they could use this list with their own teams. If no one brings it up, suggest that team leaders give this list to their current team(s) and ask team members to rate their team on each item (good, fair, poor, for example), and use the results as a springboard for team discussion and the creation of action items. (See Activity 24, *Evaluating Team Health,* for suggestions on how to lead a team self-evaluation.)

WHAT TEAMS NEED

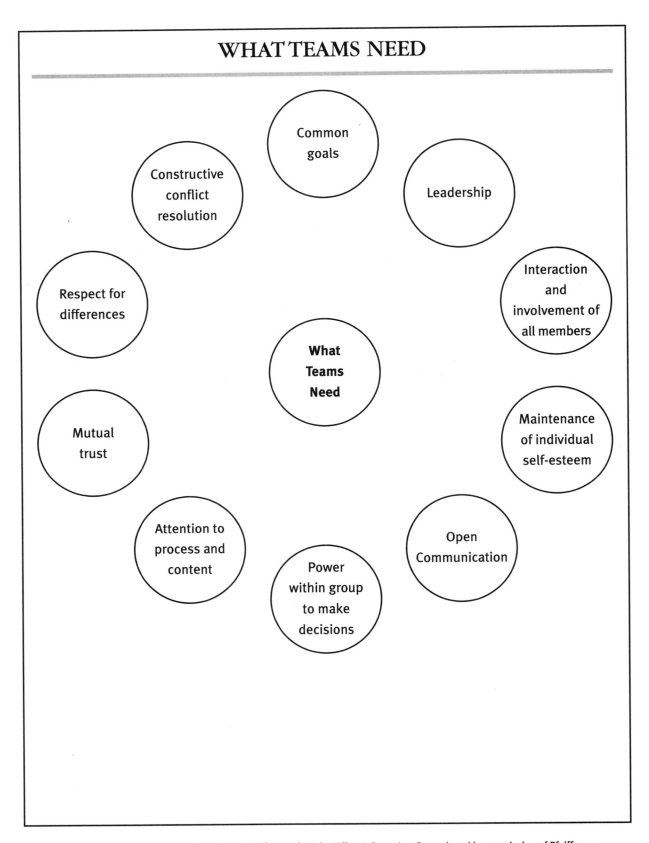

Leadership Values Auction

Purpose

- To examine individual leadership values
- To identify individual leadership values and their impact on teams

Time

2 hours

Group Size

Designed for ten to fifteen people

Materials

- Flip chart and marking pens for the facilitator
- Play money: $200,000 for each person (twenty $10,000 bills per participant)
- Two copies of the Leadership Values Sheet for each participant
- One pen/pencil for each participant
- One Leadership Values Auctioneer's Sheet for the auctioneer
- Twenty-eight 3 x 5 cards, each with a value printed on it, numbered and stacked in order from 1 through 28 (The same set can be used for both auctions)
- A flip chart and marking pen for each subgroup

Room Setup

Large semi-circle

Steps

1. *Introduce the session.* Tell the participants that they will have the chance to participate in an auction to help them clarify their own leadership values. Mention that they will have a chance later to relate these values to team leadership.

2. *Explain the auction process.* Each person will receive $200,000 of play money, which they can spend in an auction to purchase leadership values. All bidding will be done in increments of $10,000. Ask participants to imagine that they have the opportunity to become a world-renowned leader, someone who will be looked up to by many people the world over. They will, however, first need to purchase the values by which they will lead others. They can spend all of their money on one value or split it up to purchase a variety of values. They should try to use all of their money to purchase values, since any unused money is not good for any other purpose. Say that they will be given a list of values to look at before the auction begins. Each item on the list will be auctioned off. Those values they purchase will become their assets as a world-renowned leader. These will be the strengths of their leadership. They should assume that any values they do *not* purchase will be hard ones for them to acquire in the leadership challenge that is ahead of them.

3. *Give everyone the handout.* Distribute one copy of the Leadership Values Sheet to each participant along with a pencil. Ask participants to read over the sheet and take a few minutes to decide what values to bid on and how much they are willing to pay for each value.

4. *Conduct the auction.* Use the Leadership Values Auctioneer's Sheet to conduct the auction. Assign someone to collect the money and distribute the value cards. As each value is sold, distribute the 3 x 5 card with the value printed on it to the highest bidder and collect the money. Keep the pace moving quickly and try to auction off all the items. Once bidding stops, collect any money from participants that they did not use.

5. *Lead a discussion.* Once the auction is over, ask the participants to comment on the following:

- What happened as the auction proceeded?

- What went well for you?

- What frustrated you?

- Were you happy with the values you purchased? Why or why not?

- Were there any values you wished you would have purchased? Why?

- What do you wish would have happened?

- Do you think that the values you ended up with will serve you well as a world leader? Why or why not?

6. *Create a new scenario.* Explain to the group that you are going to conduct the auction a second time. The list of values will remain the same. Explain that this time, however, the leadership situation is different. You have been given the assignment of running and building a team of top nationwide experts in the field of health-care reform. Your success will be dependent on how well you get this team of experts to work collaboratively and creatively together. You are not an expert in this arena, but you are considered a top-notch team leader. During this second round of the auction, you will purchase those values that will ensure your success for leading this important team.

7. *Distribute handouts.* Distribute a second copy of the Leadership Values Sheet to each participant. Ask each participant to read the sheet again and take a few minutes to decide what values they will bid on and how much they are willing to pay for each value. Remind them that the situation is different this time. While participants are deciding how to bid, distribute $200,000 in $10,000 play money bills to each participant.

8. *Conduct the auction a second time.* Use the Leadership Values Auctioneer's Sheet as a guide.

9. *Discuss the second auction.* Divide the group into subgroups of four to five people each. Assign a subgroup leader for each subgroup to lead a discussion of the *second* auction using the following questions as a guide:

- What was different this time around?

- Did you purchase different values? Why or why not?

- Were you satisfied with the values you purchased? Why or why not?

- Do you think that the values you ended up with will serve you well as a team leader for this important nationwide team? Why or why not?

- After this discussion, what values would you bid for if you had another chance?

10. *Summarize the learning.* Stop the above discussion after twenty minutes and ask each group to list on a flip chart at least three and no more than five important things they learned from this activity. Bring the groups back together and have each group read its list out loud. Once all groups have read their lists, ask participants to comment on what they heard the most frequently.

11. *Conclude the session.* Summarize the group's findings. Focus on what values the participants felt were important in *leading a team* versus values needed for being a world-renowned leader. Ask participants to explain why these values might differ. Read over the objectives for the session. Ask how participants would change the exercise to increase what is learned.

LEADERSHIP VALUES SHEET

1. Honesty

2. Courage in the face of adversity

3. Respect for all people, regardless of ethnicity, gender, age, etc.

4. Listening to others' opinions and ideas

5. World peace

6. Decisiveness

7. Collaboration and cooperation

8. Intuition

9. Fairness and justice

10. Knowledge and experience

11. The right for people to disagree

12. The right to be authentic; the right to be "myself"

13. Creativity

14. Charisma

15. Being articulate and able to express myself well

16. Strategy and careful planning

17. Ability to persuade others

18. Having a good team of people around me

19. Personal health

20. Strong family and/or friendship ties

21. Support from powerful people

22. Faith in higher power

23. Having a mission to accomplish

24. Inspiring others

25. Getting people to work together

26. Ability to facilitate

27. Progress to a better future

28. Other people's expertise

25 Activities for Developing Team Leaders. Copyright © 2005 by John Wiley & Sons, Inc. Reproduced by permission of Pfeiffer, an Imprint of Wiley. www.pfeiffer.com

LEADERSHIP VALUES AUCTIONEER'S SHEET

Instructions: Announce the beginning of the auction. Go quickly through each item in order, saying something like:

> "Let's begin! The value is *honesty.* Do I have a bid for honesty? $10,000! $20,000! (Point to the highest bidder as you go.) Anyone want to purchase honesty for $30,000? $30,000 going, going . . . SOLD to the highest bidder for $20,000."

At this point, tell the person collecting the money to take the money from the highest bidder and hand the bidder the card with that value printed on it. Once you have said "SOLD," no one else can bid, nor can bidders change their bids. Continue as follows:

> "Next. The value is *courage in the face of adversity.* Do I have a bid for. . . ."

SECTION 2

LEAD WITH A CLEAR PURPOSE

IT IS THE TEAM LEADER'S ROLE to keep team members focused in the same direction and to motivate the team with positive, challenging, and realistic goals. The team leader must lead the process of determining the mission and goals of the team and thereafter work to keep communication clear as to how to interpret and carry out the mission and goals. Some of the things an effective team leader works with the team to do are to clarify the team's mission, to structure meetings to keep the team on track, to identify roles and responsibilities, and to develop team norms.

One of the first and foremost responsibilities of an effective team leader is to clarify the team's mission and help the team understand the boundaries of the team's work: what *is* and what is *not* within the scope of the team's responsibilities. Once a mission is established, the team leader and team members work together to identify goals that are in line with the mission. The team leader communicates, interprets, and clarifies the *organization's* goals in relation to the work of the team. In some cases, there is little room for the team leader and team members to develop or negotiate team goals. These may be mandated to the team with little room for discussion or change. Instead of the team deciding what its goals are, it can at least decide *how to achieve* those goals.

Another key team leader responsibility is to keep the team focused on its purpose when events occur that get the team off track. To focus the team and keep it on track, the team leader structures team meetings so that they are productive and achieve results that support the overall mission of the team. The team meetings are an excellent avenue for keeping the team aware of its mission and goals, for tracking progress against those goals, and for redefining and refining the team's mission and goals when necessary. When leading team meetings, the team leader must work with the team to set clear and realistic objectives for a given meeting, as well as make sure team members understand how the meeting objectives relate to overall team goals.

Another "purpose" that must be declared involves *how the team plans to work as a team.* The task of the team leader is to work with the team to identify and clarify the norms or guidelines within which it plans to operate as a team. These "team norms" become the model of how the team wants to operate and should also support the nature and specific aims of the team's mission and goals.

To help the team achieve its purpose, the team leader guides the team to define team roles and responsibilities, those roles and responsibilities that are necessary for the team to fulfill its mission and achieve its specific goals.

Some guidelines for keeping the team clear about its purpose and on track to achieve its goals are

- Involve team members as much as possible in creating and clarifying team goals;

- Keep the agreed-on goals visible to the team, discuss them often, and acknowledge clearly to the team when a goal has been met;

- Remind the team to keep the overall goals in mind when planning, implementing, making decisions, and solving problems;

- Facilitate the team to identify milestones that indicate progress toward goals. Keep these subgoals visible to all team members and facilitate the team to decide who is responsible for completion of subgoals and by what date (deadline);

- Lead the team in tracking and evaluating its own progress toward goals;

- Facilitate the team to determine if and when goals must be refined, dropped, changed, or set aside for more important goals; and

- Set clear and realistic objectives for a given meeting and make sure team members understand how the meeting objectives relate to overall team goals.

Activities in This Section

The activities in this section are designed to help team leaders build teams with clarity of purpose, defined roles and responsibilities, healthy norms of operation, and meetings that achieve specified results in relation to team goals.

Activity 6, Writing a Team Mission Statement, gives participants an opportunity to create criteria for writing an effective mission statement and to work together in subgroups to create a team mission statement. All subgroups are given the same case study and are asked to create an appropriate team mission statement. Once subgroups have created mission statements, these statements are discussed and evaluated and effective subgroup processes are noted and discussed.

Activity 7, Establishing Team Norms, helps participants understand the part norms play in team performance. During this activity, participants will participate in two subgroup activities: (1) to list healthy team norms and (2) to categorize these norms into most important, important, and less important norms. Some participants will be assigned the role of observer and will take notes as to what norms were in operation while the subgroups were working. Observers will relate their observations to the subgroups.

Activity 8, Results-Oriented Meetings, teaches participants the difference between meeting *agendas* and meeting *objectives* and stresses the importance of building a meeting around results-oriented meeting objectives. Participants are given guidelines for recognizing and writing results-oriented meeting objectives. They then work in pairs to write one or two results-oriented meeting objectives for real-world meeting situations. These objectives are posted, and the participants review each objective based on a set of criteria.

Activity 9, Team Roles: Using the Affinity Diagram, gives participants a chance to identify and describe the responsibilities of various team roles, using an Affinity Diagram. Participants brainstorm ideas individually, work in a group to arrange the ideas into categories while remaining silent, and finally finish arranging and formulating the ideas while discussing them aloud. This activity allows participants to further understand team roles and responsibilities, while experiencing and learning about an effective team tool, the Affinity Diagram.

Writing a Team Mission Statement

Purpose

- To understand what an effective mission statement is and its value to a team
- To develop guidelines for creating an effective mission statement
- To experience and evaluate the task of creating a team mission statement

Time

2 1/2 hours

Group Size

Eight to twenty-four people, enough for two or more teams of from four to five people each

Materials

- Flip chart and marking pens for the facilitator
- Flip chart paper and marking pens for each team
- Prepared flip chart showing criteria for an effective team mission statement (see Step 2)
- One copy of the Sheer Beauty Team Case Study per person
- One copy of the Writing a Team Mission Statement Observer Sheet for each observer

- One copy of Evaluating Team Mission Statements for each participant
- A calculator
- Masking tape

Room Setup

A room with several small tables that will seat four or five people per table, or a U-shape setup that will accommodate small teams (see diagram on page 22)

Steps

1. *Explain the goals of the session and introduce the topic.* Lead a discussion of the following questions:

    - What is a team mission statement?

    - What is the purpose and value of a team mission statement?

    - What makes an effective team mission statement?

    List all the ideas concisely and as close to the wording of the participants as possible.

2. *Review the criteria for a good team mission statement.* Next, post the prepared flip chart with criteria for an effective team mission statement and briefly explain the meaning of each criterion:

```
CRITERIA
The team mission statement:
• is clear and to the point
• is memorable
• is inspiring
• fits the team's needs
```

Ask the group if there are other important criteria for a good team mission statement. Add these to the list.

3. *Have subgroups work on suggestions for developing a mission statement.* Divide the group into subgroups of from four or five people each. Instruct each subgroup to come up with *suggestions to teams for developing a mission statement.* In other words, how should a team go about creating its mission statement? Instruct subgroups to write their suggestions on a flip chart and post them in the room.

4. *Reconvene the large group.* After about 15 minutes bring everyone together and ask a spokesperson from each subgroup to read its suggestions. When the subgroups are finished, ask the group members to comment on these suggestions: Are they reasonable? Workable? Any problems? Are they willing to use these ideas to write their own mission statements? Note those suggestions that the participants think they would use to write a team mission statement.

5. *Develop team mission statements.* The goal of this step is for each subgroup to write what the mission of the Sheer Beauty Team should be. Distribute a copy of the Sheer Beauty Team Case Study, which describes a fictitious team in need of a clear mission statement, and a pen or pencil to each participant and ask them to read the case.

    Divide the group into subgroups of from four to five people each. Instruct the subgroups to use the suggestions highlighted from the previous exercise to develop and write a mission statement for the team in the case study. Select one person from each subgroup to be an observer for this process. Call observers aside and give them copies of the Writing a Team Mission Statement Observer Sheet. Instruct them to observe their subgroup and answer the questions on the sheet. Ask observers to rejoin their respective groups. After 30 to 40 minutes, instruct the subgroups to write their finished team mission statements (even if it is still in rough draft) on a flip chart and post it somewhere in the room.

6. *Debrief the process.* Reconvene the large group, and ask each subgroup to present its statement. After all subgroups have presented their statement, ask the observers to report on the following:

    - What suggestions (from the first part of the exercise) seemed to work the best?

    - What did your subgroup do particularly well?

    - What could your subgroup have done differently to produce a better mission statement?

Next, ask the subgroup members to comment on the following questions:

- What was the experience of writing another team's mission statement like?

- What suggestions (from the first part of the exercise) did you use? How well did they work?

- What did your group do particularly well?

- What did you learn about writing a team mission statement?

7. *Review the team mission statements.* Go around to each posted mission statement and assign a letter to each one (A, B, C, D, etc.). Distribute a copy of the Evaluating Team Mission Statements handout to each person and instruct all participants (including observers) to go to each statement in the room, read it, and complete the evaluation.

8. *Tally the results.* Go around the room for each mission statement and ask for the *total points* each person assigned it. Write each person's total points on a flip chart next to the letter that represents the mission statement. Next, total the points for each mission statement. (Ask for someone in the room to use a calculator to help you.) If one or two mission statements clearly stand out, ask the subgroups that created those statements to share briefly what worked particularly well for the group, what suggestions were used, etc.

9. *Wrap up the session.* Go around the room and ask each person to relate *one important thing* he or she learned during the session that can be put to use on his or her own teams. Ask someone to volunteer to copy the guidelines generated by the group and distribute them via e-mail to everyone in the session. Ask for feedback on the session (See "Managing the Group Training Session" in the Introduction, page 11) and adjourn the group.

Variation

Write a mission statement for one of the participant's team. To do so, allow the group to ask questions of that person to gain information necessary to write a mission statement.

SHEER BEAUTY TEAM CASE STUDY

Mary-Eileen Lorsworth is the director of an organization that develops, manufactures, and distributes a line of products called Sheer Beauty for a large cosmetic corporation. Lorsworth has been forward thinking in her approach to implementing high performing teams in the organization. She has encouraged and rewarded teamwork and has developed a culture where team members and team leaders work collaboratively to make decisions, initiate change, ensure quality, and plan details of the team's work. For the most part, people in the organization feel empowered to make suggestions, speak up about problems, and alert management to how the company can improve its overall performance. One thing most people appreciate is that the team is allowed to set its own standards of operation as long as the work gets done. The team has done quite well and managed to meet its production and profit goals for the larger corporation.

However, over the past few months, it has been brought to Lorsworth's attention by several of her top team leaders that the organization is suffering some setbacks and problems as a result of various teams not working in concert. True, teams have been able to get a lot accomplished; however, due to problems in cross-team and cross-functional communication and cooperation, some important tasks are falling through the cracks. What's worse, team leaders have reported, they are beginning to receive feedback from customers that delivery and quality problems are increasing and that it is more and more difficult to work through problems with the organization. Sometimes, the customer does not know whom to call or go to with a concern. It seems that frequently there is confusion about who owns what problem. One other problem Lorsworth knows is that the Chemistry Department's manager fosters secrecy within Research and Development ranks and that it is difficult for marketing and sales to obtain accurate information as to when new products will be available for distribution to customers.

Lorsworth has decided to create a top-level, cross-functional team to address these problems. She will ask the head of each major department to serve on the team, along with a representative from each of the three outside firms that distribute and create the advertising for Sheer Beauty's cosmetic line. Her instincts tell her that unless her organization's top influencers function as a high-performing team, the above-mentioned problems will continue to worsen.

WRITING A TEAM MISSION STATEMENT
OBSERVER SHEET

Instructions: As you observe your subgroup, answer as many of the following questions as you can and note any other observations you think are significant:

1. Did the group follow some or all of the guidelines?

2. What guidelines worked well?

3. What guidelines did not work well? Why was that?

4. What other processes did the group use? Were they successful? Why or why not?

5. Did all members of the group participate? Was participation balanced?

6. Did someone take a team leader role or did the group work without a leader?

7. What did the group do particularly well?

8. What could the group have done differently to increase efficiency or produce a better team mission statement?

EVALUATING TEAM MISSION STATEMENTS

Instructions: For each of the mission statements, assign from 1 to 3 points for each of the four questions. Use the following point scale:

Not really = 1 point   Somewhat = 2 points   Very = 3 points

Total the points you gave to each mission statement.

Mission Statement A

Points

_____ Is the statement *clear* and *to the point*?

_____ Is it *memorable* enough for a team member to tell it to someone outside his or her team?

_____ Is it *inspiring*? Does it make you really want to stretch to achieve it?

_____ Does it fit the *organization's needs*?

_____ TOTAL POINTS

Mission Statement B

Points

_____ Is the statement *clear* and *to the point*?

_____ Is it *memorable* enough for a team member to tell it to someone outside his or her team?

_____ Is it *inspiring*? Does it make you really want to stretch to achieve it?

_____ Does it fit the *organization's needs*?

_____ TOTAL POINTS

Mission Statement C

Points

_____ Is the statement *clear* and *to the point*?

_____ Is it *memorable* enough for a team member to tell it to someone outside his or her team?

_____ Is it *inspiring*? Does it make you really want to stretch to achieve it?

_____ Does it fit the *organization's needs*?

_____ TOTAL POINTS

Mission Statement D

Points

_____ Is the statement *clear* and *to the point*?

_____ Is it *memorable* enough for a team member to tell it to someone outside his or her team?

_____ Is it *inspiring*? Does it make you really want to stretch to achieve it?

_____ Does it fit the *organization's needs*?

_____ TOTAL POINTS

Mission Statement E

Points

_____ Is the statement *clear* and *to the point*?

_____ Is it *memorable* enough for a team member to tell it to someone outside his or her team?

_____ Is it *inspiring*? Does it make you really want to stretch to achieve it?

_____ Does it fit the *organization's needs*?

_____ TOTAL POINTS

Mission Statement F

Points

_____ Is the statement *clear* and *to the point*?

_____ Is it *memorable* enough for a team member to tell it to someone outside his or her team?

_____ Is it *inspiring*? Does it make you want to stretch to achieve it?

_____ Does it fit the *organization's needs*?

_____ TOTAL POINTS

Establishing Team Norms

Purpose

- To understand norms of group behavior and the part norms play in team performance
- To learn and experience a process of setting team norms
- To observe and identify team norms in operation

Time

1 1/2 to 2 hours

Group Size

Designed for twelve to twenty people

Materials

- Flip chart and marking pens for the facilitator
- Pen/pencil for each person
- Establishing Team Norms handout for each participant
- Establishing Team Norms Observer Sheet for each observer
- A flip chart and marking pens for each team

Room Setup

U-shape (see diagram on page 22)

Steps

1. *Introduce the session and discuss the concept of team norms.* Explain the purpose of the session. Ask the group what is meant by the term "team norms." Thank the participants for their insights and post the definition of norms on a flip chart, as follows:

   Norms: the standards of conduct that regulate the behavior of the individual members of a team or a group of people.

   Other terms for "norms" are guidelines, governing principles, or standards of behavior that characterize a group. Explain that when people work and/or live together (such as in families, organizations, teams, etc.) there are standards of behavior that govern their interactions and actions. These standards generally develop over time and eventually define the "personality" or characteristics of a group or culture.

   Ask the group to give you some examples of norms for the following:

   - The company they currently work in

   - Drivers in their city or town

   - The American culture; norms of other cultures such Japanese, Italian, etc.

   - A team they are currently on

   Mention that there can be healthy, as well as unhealthy, norms. Ask the group to name a couple of examples of healthy team norms and a couple of unhealthy team norms. List the responses.

   Explain that a team, or any group or organization, has a choice to (1) let the norms develop naturally over time, or (2) select the norms they desire and monitor them to ensure people hold to those standards. Ask the participants, "What can happen when norms are allowed to develop naturally over time?" List the responses. Draw out some of the disadvantages to letting norms just happen:

   - Bad habits develop

   - Dominant or more charismatic people may override quieter, less assertive ones

- There may be no clear "rules" for behavior, and people may be uncertain and confused

- Opportunities to make progress may be hindered by ineffective norms

Point out that communities, states, and nations generally try to select the standards they desire and motivate citizens by enforcing the "laws" set up to protect the standards. Also, people tend to prefer knowing what standards are expected of them up-front so they don't inadvertently let the group down or fail to adhere to important group norms.

Mention that norms are a critical part of a team's life and that, whether the norms are agreed on up-front or they develop over time, there *will be* team norms. It is up to the team leader to guide the team in establishing, reviewing, and revising its norms so that the goals of the team can be achieved and the team can function in a satisfying way for its members.

2. *Introduce the activity.* Distribute the Establishing Team Norms handout. Explain that the group will be divided into teams and that each team will create a list of *healthy team norms,* using the handout as a starting point. Each team should appoint a recorder to list the norms large enough for all to see. They may need to use more than one piece of flip chart paper. Tell the group that each team will have an observer who will report his or her observations later in the session. The observer and the team being observed should not interact during the activity.

3. *Divide the group into teams.* Put five or six people in each group and assign one person from each team to be an observer. Ask the teams to find places in the room to assemble, get markers and flip chart paper, and read over the handout. *Ask them not to begin until the observers are ready.*

4. *Give the observers their assignment.* Assemble the observers into an area of the room and give them copies of the Establishing Team Norms Observer Sheet. Do not let the teams hear your instructions to the observers. Explain to the observers that they will be watching the teams to determine their norms or standards of behavior as a team. They can use the list of norms on the Establishing Team Norms Observer Sheet as examples, and they can add any of their own.

5. *Conduct the first part of the activity.* Tell the teams they will have 15 to 20 minutes to come up with a list of norms. Monitor the teams so

they have adequate time to list their norms. If they need some more time, extend the time. Stop this part of the activity when the energy dies down. Ask each team to leave its list posted in the area where it was working.

6. *Debrief the first part of the activity.* Bring the group back together. Going from one team to the next, ask each observer to comment on the norms he or she saw in operation as his or her team was working. Ask the team members who were observed if they were aware of any of these norms and what they thought of the way their team was working. Ask the observer and the team what, if any, standards of behavior might improve that team's process. Do this for each of the teams.

7. *Conduct the second part of the activity.* Instruct the teams and observers to return to their areas and to make *three separate flip charts* and label them (1) Most Important Norms, (2) Important Norms, and (3) Less Important Norms. Each team's assignment is to take each of the norms they listed earlier and put them into one of the categories or "buckets." Tell the teams to aim for a fairly equal distribution of their norms among the three categories. They should try to have agreement on the team as to where each norm belongs. If they cannot reach agreement, the recorder should circle the norm on the original list that team members did not agree on. The observers will once again observe the teams working and make notes. (Use the same observers as before, since they will be comparing the two parts of the activity.) Observers should not interact with the team at all. After about 30 minutes, ask each team to select a spokesperson to present the categories and norms decided on.

8. *Debrief the experience.* Bring the group back together and, one team at a time, do the following:

   - Have the spokesperson report the decision of the team by reading off each category and the items in it.

   - Ask the observer for that team to report on the norms he or she saw that were the most operative during the second part of the activity.

   - Ask the team and the observer to comment on whether and how the norms changed from the first to the second part of the activity. Ask, "Why did the changes occur?" Ask, "What did the team learn from the experience?"

9. *Conclude the session.* Once all the teams have reported, ask the group if it would like someone to distribute the lists from all the teams to all the participants. If so, ask for a volunteer to do so and make sure he or she has an e-mail or mail address to use for each participant. If desired, ask for feedback on the session (see "Managing the Group Training Session" in the Introduction, page 11) and adjourn the group.

ESTABLISHING TEAM NORMS

Below are a few examples of norms that you might choose for your team. Some of the areas for which you may wish to create team norms are meetings, communication, sharing of information, and team confidentialities.

1. Be present at all team meetings.

2. Hear one another out.

3. Be aware of the roles and responsibilities of other team members.

4. Alert team members to unforeseen problems in a timely way.

ESTABLISHING TEAM NORMS OBSERVER SHEET

First Round

Instructions: Put a check mark beside each behavior when you see it occurring in the team you are observing. Place an asterisk beside those behaviors that occur frequently enough to call them a "norm."

Healthy Behaviors

_____ Team members listen carefully to one another/hear one another out.

_____ Team members' ideas are all recorded.

_____ Team members encourage one another to clarify ideas.

_____ There is a balance of participation.

_____ Team members feel free to ask questions or make suggestions.

_____ Disagreements are discussed calmly.

_____ Team members are allowed to express a variety of opinions.

_____ Other healthy norms you observed:

Unhealthy Behaviors

_____ Team members interrupt one another.

_____ Not all ideas are recorded.

_____ Those with different opinions are ignored.

_____ Disagreements are put down or ignored.

_____ Dominant members take over; quieter members withdraw.

_____ Other unhealthy behaviors:

Second Round

Instructions: Put a check mark beside each behavior when you see it occurring in the team you are observing. Place an asterisk beside those behaviors that occur frequently enough to call them a "norm."

Healthy Behaviors

_____ Team members listen carefully to one another/hear one another out.

_____ Team members' ideas are all recorded.

_____ Team members encourage one another to clarify ideas.

_____ There is a balance of participation.

_____ Team members feel free to ask questions or make suggestions.

_____ Disagreements are discussed calmly.

_____ Team members are allowed to express a variety of opinions.

_____ Other healthy norms you observed:

Unhealthy Behaviors

_____ Team members interrupt one another.

_____ Not all ideas are recorded.

_____ Those with different opinions are ignored.

_____ Disagreements are put down or ignored.

_____ Dominant members take over; quieter members withdraw.

_____ Other unhealthy behaviors:

ACTIVITY 8

Results-Oriented Meetings

Purpose

- To help team leaders distinguish between meeting *agendas* and meeting *objectives*
- To help team leaders understand the pitfalls of leading a meeting without clear, results-oriented meeting objectives
- To give team leaders practice in writing and evaluating meeting objectives

Time

1 1/2 to 2 hours

Group Size

Ten to twelve people

Materials

- One Objectives: The Driving Force handout per person
- Paper and pen/pencil for each pair
- Flip chart paper and marking pens for each pair
- Flip chart and marking pens for the facilitator

Room Setup

U-shape (see diagram on page 22)

Steps

1. *Introduce the session.* Introduce the topic by explaining the importance of having clear and results-oriented meeting objectives. A suggested introduction:

   > "To design and facilitate a successful meeting, the facilitator must focus
   > the group on the desired end result of the meeting or the goal for the
   > meeting. An effective way to do this is to write the meeting objective(s)
   > on a flip chart and post it for all to see. Whether the objective is decided
   > before the meeting begins or at the beginning of the meeting, it should
   > be results-oriented and posted. Clear, realistic, and relevant objectives
   > will keep the group energized and focused as it moves toward achieving
   > something by the end of the meeting. During this activity, we will learn
   > to recognize and write a results-oriented meeting objective. First let's
   > discuss the difference between the meeting agenda and the objectives."

2. *Discuss the term "Meeting Agenda."* Begin by asking the group, "What
   is an agenda for a meeting?" List all responses on a flip chart. There
   may be some disagreement. Point out that the dictionary defines
   agenda as "a list, plan, or outline of things to be done, matters to be
   acted upon or voted upon." Explain that the agenda is generally the
   list of topics or activities to be covered during a meeting and is presented in the time sequence of how the meeting will flow. It may or
   may not include times and people in charge of the various activities.
   An agenda may or may not be presented along with the objective(s)
   or anticipated outcomes for the meeting.

3. *Distinguish between an Agenda and Objectives.* Emphasize that it is
   important for team leaders to be able to distinguish between *objectives* for a meeting and the *agenda* for a meeting. Objectives are the
   goals for the meeting, the end product aimed for. The agenda is the
   flow of activities and/or topics to support the achievement of those
   objectives. When planning a meeting, the team leader must first determine the meeting's objectives or the desired end result of the meeting. The agenda is planned *after* the objectives and is designed to
   support those objectives. (For further discussion of agenda and objectives, refer to pages 143–147 in *How to LEAD Work Teams: Facilitation Skills,* as listed in the Reference section.)

4. *Review the handout.* Distribute Objectives: The Driving Force and explain the diagram, noting that all aspects of a meeting and decisions about how the meeting should unfold should be determined by the objectives of the meeting. The objectives determine:

- Whether the meeting is necessary (spoke #1 on the wheel)
- Who should attend the meeting (spoke #2)
- When and how long the meeting should be (spoke #3)
- Where the meeting should be (spoke #4)
- Whether there should be any pre-meeting work (spoke #5)
- What processes and agenda will be used (spoke #6)
- What adjustments are needed during the meeting (spoke #7)
- And finally, and most importantly, whether the meeting was successful (spoke #8)

5. *Show examples of results-oriented meeting objectives.* Explain that a results-oriented objective contains three parts:

- *An Action:* What the group will be doing during the meeting.
- *An Outcome:* What the result of that action will be.
- *Qualifiers:* Descriptive words or phrases to focus the group.

Give a few examples, such as:

- Decide which alternative will benefit us the most. "Decide" is the action; "which alternative" is the outcome; "will benefit us the most" is the qualifier.
- Plan the next steps we will take on the Avondale project. "Plan" is the action; "the next steps" is the outcome; "we will take on the Avondale project" is the qualifier.

For an objective to be results-oriented, the group must walk away with some tangible result (or outcome) from the meeting. Tangible results in the above examples were an alternative selected (first example) and the next steps on a project identified (second example). If a meeting has no tangible outcome, it is difficult to show that it was a successful meeting. There are common "actions" that take place in meetings that do not result in tangible outcomes. These actions do not lead directly to outcomes, although they may be part of the process of the meeting. Some examples of common actions that are not part of the results-oriented objective are

- *Discuss:* This is a common action in meetings. However, discussing does not lead to a defined outcome.

- *Update:* Informing people may be a necessary part of a meeting, but it doesn't have a tangible result.

- *Review:* Reviewing progress or data may be necessary but should not be the end outcome of a results-oriented meeting.

Explain that meetings must include updates, discussions, and reviews, but that the end goal of a meeting should be more than that. Meetings should have a results-oriented objective that identifies some tangible result. Words like "discuss," "update," and "review" are generally not part of the stated results-oriented objective.

6. *Create examples.* Ask the group to come up with a few examples of results-oriented objectives and write these examples on a flip chart. As these are suggested, ask the group to identify the Action, Outcome and Qualifiers for each objective it creates. Here are a few more examples of results-oriented objectives:

- List the tasks to be completed before implementation.

- Brainstorm the possible causes of equipment failure.

- Determine which software program meets our established criteria.

- Rewrite the existing procedures for handling customer merchandise returns.

- Outline the steps we will take to improve customer service.

- List and prioritize the department's goals for the upcoming year.

7. *Write meeting objectives.* Instruct the participants that they are going to write some meeting objectives for the types of meetings they have in their organization(s). Divide the group into pairs, hand out paper and pens or pencils, and instruct the pairs as follows:

- Write two different and typical meeting situations that call for results-oriented meeting objectives. Write these on a piece of paper.

- Trade your pair's two situations with another pair's two situations.

- Write one or two results-oriented meeting objectives for *each* of the meeting situations your pair receives.

- Post the objectives your pair has written.

8. *Discuss meeting objectives.* Ask someone from each pair to read the meeting situation and the objective(s) the pair created for that situation. After each objective is read, ask the presenter to identify the Action, Outcome, and Qualifier for each objective. Ask the group:

   - Is this a clear, results-oriented objective for the situation?

   - If you were present at this meeting, would you be clear about what the group was trying to accomplish at this meeting?

   - Would you be motivated to work on this objective?

   If someone does not think the objective meets all of these criteria, ask that person and/or the group for suggestions that would make it better. Go to the flip chart and revise the objective as suggested by the group. Before changing any words, however, check with the pair who created the original objective to make sure the suggestions are appropriate for the situation it received. Once an objective has been revised, ask the pair who wrote the original objective if it agrees that the revised objective better meets the criteria. Continue going over each objective until each pair's objectives have been discussed and revised, if necessary.

9. *Conclude the session.* Ask someone to briefly describe the difference between a meeting *agenda* and meeting *objectives,* and reinforce the importance of using results-oriented objectives to focus the team meeting and leave everyone with a feeling of success once the identified objectives are met. Read the objectives for the session and point out that the group accomplished the purpose of the session. If desired, ask for feedback on the session (See Managing the Group Training Session, page 11) and adjourn the group.

Reference

Rees, F. (2001). *How to LEAD Work Teams: Facilitation Skills* (2nd ed.) San Francisco: Pfeiffer.

OBJECTIVES: THE DRIVING FORCE

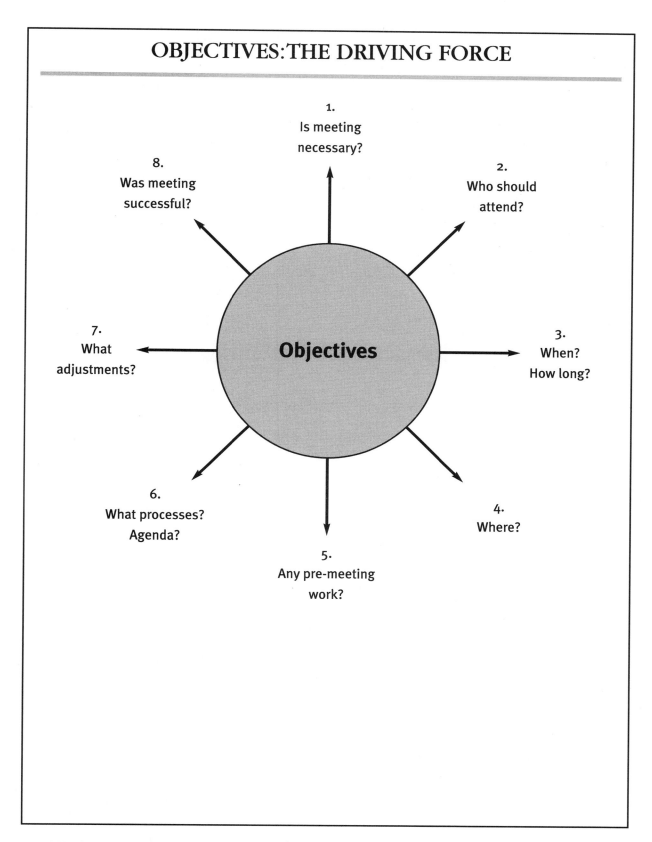

1.
Is meeting
necessary?

2.
Who should
attend?

3.
When?
How long?

4.
Where?

5.
Any pre-meeting
work?

6.
What processes?
Agenda?

7.
What
adjustments?

8.
Was meeting
successful?

Objectives

Team Roles:
Using the Affinity Diagram

Purpose

- To identify and describe the roles needed for a team to function effectively
- To experience using the Affinity Diagram as a team tool

Time

1 1/2 to 2 hours

Group Size

Designed for twelve to sixteen people

Materials

- Several 3 x 5 sticky notes (ten to twelve) for each participant, plus extras
- One black marking pen (medium point) for each participant
- A large table (or two tables) for organizing the sticky notes (for the Affinity Diagram); divide the table into five sections and label the sections: Team Leader, Team Member, Facilitator, Recorder, and Other
- One copy of the Team Roles Handout per participant
- Flip chart and marking pens for the facilitator

Room Setup

U-shape (see diagram on page 22)

Steps

1. *Introduce the session.* Go over the purpose of the session. Tell the participants that, as team leaders, they are responsible for making sure that everyone understands his or her role on the team. Tell the participants that in today's session, they will identify typical team roles and responsibilities so that team leaders will have a "template" or guideline to work with when they return to their teams. Mention that the roles they will identify will be *generic* and that, since every team is different in the real world, each team may have to adapt these guidelines to meet its own needs.

2. *Define "team role."* Post the following definition of "team role" and ask the participants if this is an adequate definition of "team role." If not, ask the participants to help you come up with a clear definition to work from.

   > Team Role—a set of tasks and/or responsibilities that helps the team do its work and operate effectively as a team. A team role may be filled by one or more individuals on the team (*example:* meeting facilitator).

   Ask the participants to come up with some other examples of team roles (e.g., team leader, sponsor, recorder, and so on). List these on a flip chart for all to see. Explain that it is important for team members to understand each of the team roles and to agree on the tasks and responsibilities of each. If there is disagreement, confusion, or too much overlap of roles, there will be problems and inefficiencies on the team. Lack of role clarity can cause a team to struggle and even to fail.

3. *Introduce the activity.* Distribute the sticky notes and marking pens. Tell participants that they are going to brainstorm individually and silently. Write and post this statement on a flip chart for all to see:

   > Brainstorm all the tasks and responsibilities you can think of that a team must carry out. Write one idea on each sticky note.

   Encourage participants not to analyze or judge their ideas, but to jot them down *quickly.* Ask them to *print* as *legibly* as possible. Have plenty of sticky notes handy if participants run out. Tell the participants they will be given 10 minutes to write as many ideas as they can. Tell them to keep their completed sticky notes with them, but suggest they tear them off as they go to make writing on them easier. Ask if there are any questions. If necessary, give one or two examples of a team task or responsibility (use the Team Roles Handout for ideas).

4. *Start the brainstorming session.* Tell participants to begin and allow 10 minutes. Coach them as they write if necessary: keep the ideas going, don't analyze, the more ideas the better, anything goes, etc. Tell them not to worry about spelling or grammar; abbreviations are all right but should not be overdone or the ideas will be hard to read. While participants are working, make sure the large table is prepared as explained in the Materials section. Call time after 10 minutes.

5. *Begin creating the Affinity Diagram.* Tell the participants to gather their ideas and to remain *silent.* Ask them to group around the large table and to place each of their items under the role title (team leader, team member, facilitator, recorder, other) that they think is the *most responsible* for the task or responsibility. If they think the item belongs under more than one role, tell them to place it under the role that is *most* responsible. Remind them *not to talk* during this portion of the activity. Duplicate ideas can be clustered together.

6. *Revise the Affinity Diagram (remaining silent).* Once everyone has placed his or her items on the table, tell the participants to remain silent and to read what others have put down. Tell the participants that they can now move any of the items to other categories if they wish. They should remain silent. They can move either their own items or others' items to different categories. The purpose is to think about what tasks and responsibilities belong to each role. Call time after a few minutes. Watch the group to determine when participants are ready to move on (either when the energy dies down or when it is evident that disagreements over where certain items belong will not be settled while the group remains silent).

7. *Revise the Affinity Diagram (talking).* Tell the participants that they no longer need to remain silent but can now discuss aloud where the items go. Instruct the group to work together to do the following: (1) come to consensus on where the tasks and responsibilities belong; (2) add any missing tasks or responsibilities; and (3) set aside any items on which the group cannot come to agreement. They can use the "Other" category for any stray items, or they can come up with other roles for these items, if necessary. Allow 15 to 20 minutes for

this portion of the activity (longer if the group needs it). If you are not certain when to call time, ask the participants if they are ready to stop and discuss what they have done.

8. *Discuss the activity.* Bring the participants back to their seats and use the following questions to stimulate discussion:

   - What happened during the *silent* time when you were placing your ideas on the table? What was helpful about remaining silent? What was difficult? How was creativity stimulated or hindered during the silent portion? How were conflicts resolved?

   - What happened when you could *talk* about where the items belonged? What was helpful or difficult about being allowed to talk? How were conflicts resolved?

   - How do you feel about the quality of the work you did on the Affinity Diagram? Do you believe the lists you made are fairly complete? Why or why not? Is there more work to be done? If so, what?

9. *Distribute the Team Roles Handout.* Tell the group that the handout represents a compilation of ideas accumulated over several years from work with teams, consultants, trainers, team leaders, and members in many different types of organizations. It is meant as a guide only and is a *generic* list. Teams may have to revise these lists to meet their specific needs. Ask the group to look at the list and compare it to what they put together in the Affinity Diagram. Post the following questions and read them aloud:

   - Are the lists similar or different?

   - Are there any major discrepancies? What are they?

Have the participants get up and go to the table to compare the lists and think about their answers to the questions. Tell them they are free to discuss the lists at this time. After a few minutes, bring the group back together and lead a discussion on the questions posted. Ask for a volunteer to copy the Affinity Diagram lists generated by the group and send everyone a copy. Ask the group how they are likely to use the information they learned today in working out the roles in their teams.

This may be a good time to point out that role assignments need not be static for a team to function well. In a high performing team, team members may readily switch or double up on roles so the team functions at an optimum level of performance at all times. This type of role switching has to be done with the team and team leader in agreement about how roles are shared or passed on to others. On any team, how-ever, it is important that—at a given point in time—every team member is clear about the role he or she is filling.

10. *Discuss the Affinity Diagram process.* Ask participants to focus on the process they used to come up with the responsibilities and tasks for each team role. Tell them that the process they experienced is called an Affinity Diagram, and it is one tool for helping a group reach consensus. Ask them to comment on the following questions:

   - What was effective about the process?
   - What is the purpose of the individual brainstorming time?
   - What is the purpose of remaining silent during the first placement of ideas into groupings?
   - What disadvantages do you see in using this process?
   - What, when, and how might you use this process in your team?

   Suggest a few ways if no one has any suggestions, such as to identify and group tasks for a major project or to categorize a large list of brainstormed ideas.

11. *Wrap up the session.* Review the purpose of the session, get feedback on the activity (see "Managing the Group Training Session: Tips for Trainers" in the Introduction, page 11), and adjourn.

TEAM ROLES HANDOUT

Team Leader

Role: Manage and coordinate the team so that it gets its best work done, provide resources to the team, link the team and its work to the rest of the organization, and be an active team member.

  Tasks: Some of the tasks the team leader performs are

- Report team progress to the sponsor or others outside the team.
- Set up team meetings, notify team members, secure facility and supplies, and see that team meetings are effective.
- Keep the team focused on what it is supposed to be doing.
- Define boundaries for the team: what the team is expected/not expected to do.
- Keep open channels of communication between the team and the larger organization.
- Act as a project manager for the work of the team.
- Procure resources for the team (facilitator, supplies, subject-matter experts, funding).
- Clarify the organization's expectations of the team.
- Explain and, if necessary, defend the process the team is using to do its work.
- Ensure team productivity.
- Contribute to the work of the team (as a team member) without dominating or over-influencing, without "pulling rank."
- Make sure team members are clear about their individual action items and commitments.
- Make sure team efforts are documented and made available as needed to the team.

Team Facilitator

Role: Give the team processes and structure in which to do its best work. Lead the team's meetings, when needed, so that the best decisions are reached. Manage the process of group discussion and help the team understand its own needs and dynamics. Guide the team in making the changes necessary to become a cohesive team. Be the recorder during group discussions or help the recorder carry out his or her role. *It is critical that the facilitator understand the importance of and use of the recorded data.* Help the leader and the team set and keep to realistic time frames for completion of team activities.

  Tasks: Some of the tasks the team facilitator performs are

- Help the team leader plan the initial team meetings.
- Facilitate the team meetings.
- Model and teach productive meeting behaviors and processes.
- Guide the team until it becomes adept at planning its own meetings.

- Encourage open channels of communication among the team members and between the team and the larger organization.
- Facilitate the team in evaluating its own progress as a team.
- Suggest group processes that will help the team do its best work.

The facilitator usually plays the key role in leading the team's meetings. This involves many tasks, such as:

- See that the team uses the most effective methods to do its work, with time to consider ideas and alternatives.
- Select from a variety of group process tools and methods, depending on what the work and the team's experience call for.
- Remain neutral on the content of the team's meeting, while taking an active role in guiding the process.
- Draw out everyone and balance the participation as much as possible.
- Encourage dialogue among team members, not between the facilitator and the team members. (This usually means simply being quiet and allowing team members to respond to one another.)
- Ensure that different points of view have been aired and considered.
- Record, organize, and summarize inputs of the team; post these in front of the room so all can see.
- Manage meeting time wisely. (As the meeting progresses, let the team know where they stand on time. When the team is planning its next meeting, give the team feedback on how long certain agenda items have taken in the past. Give the team a warning when it is going over the allotted time on a particular item, or when it is nearing the designated ending time for the meeting.)
- Listen actively to all team members.
- If someone else is recording, make suggestions to the recorder when necessary, such as asking the recorder to label a flip chart, number items, post flip charts, or capture an idea that was overlooked.

Team Member

Role: Contribute knowledge, experience, time, and support to both the team's work and the building of a cohesive team, so that the mutually agreed on goals of the team are achieved.

    Tasks: Some of the tasks the team member performs are

- Attend team meetings.
- Contribute to team meeting discussions and decisions in a productive, positive way.
- Carry out action items and assignments as promised to the team.
- Offer support to other team members.
- Ask questions and listen to teammates.
- Share relevant information with the team.

- Help the team leader, facilitator, and sponsor in their roles.

- Speak up with own opinions and feelings, make suggestions, and ask important questions of the team.

- Don't hold up team progress by repeating ideas over and over. Let them ride on their own merit.

- Use professional skills and experience (e.g., organizing abilities, computer knowledge, technical expertise, people skills, etc.) to help the team be productive.

- Contribute to the work of the team without dominating or over-influencing.

- Make an effort to hear and understand teammates' points of view.

- Remove blocks and barriers to the team's success, when possible.

Team Sponsor (Coach, Champion, Mentor, Advisor)

Role: Provide overall direction, support, and encouragement to the team and ensure that the team's efforts support organization goals. Act as an advisor to the team when needed, or run interference for the team in the rest of the organization. Coach and collaborate with the team leader to set clear boundaries for the team, as well as give the team necessary leeway and authority to get its work done. Be available to the team as a resource.

   Tasks: Some of the tasks the team sponsor performs are

- Attend team meetings from time to time; show support.

- Find resources for the team when needed.

- Coach, encourage, and support the team leader.

- Help team leader define team boundaries.

- Open channels of communication between the team and the larger organization.

- Keep the team leader informed of information and/or changes in the organization that may impact the team's work or its goals.

- Clarify the organization's expectations of the team.

- Explain and, if necessary, defend the process the team is using to get its work done.

- Remove blocks and barriers to the team's success, when possible.

Team Recorder

Generally this role works best when merged with the facilitator role, but for some teams it works best to have both a facilitator *and* a recorder.

   Role: Record key points in the discussions and decisions of a team.

   Tasks: Some of the tasks the team recorder might need to perform are

- Remain silent on the content of the discussion.

- Accurately record key words and phrases, as close to the speaker's words as possible (so as not to alter the intended meaning).

25 Activities for Developing Team Leaders. Copyright © 2005 by John Wiley & Sons, Inc. Reproduced by permission of Pfeiffer, an Imprint of Wiley. www.pfeiffer.com

- Write legibly and large enough for all to see.

- If necessary, ask a team member to summarize comments so they can be recorded.

- Get help with spelling, if needed.

- Organize the data so it can be used efficiently by the group (e.g., title the charts, show where each different idea begins, indent, number points, use bullets, arrows—whatever helps the group see the relationship of the material).

- Tear off and hang the charts so they can be referred to as needed. Get help posting them, if necessary.

- Be careful not to leave out someone's idea or point.

- Know when to sit down and let the group discuss without recording. It isn't possible or necessary to record every point.

- Organize the charts and see that they are documented and copied for every team member's use.

SECTION 3

EMPOWER PEOPLE
TO PARTICIPATE

THE TRUE POWER OF TEAMWORK comes from the fullest possible participation of every team member. It is the role of the team leader to allow ample opportunity for team members to be involved in deciding, planning, implementing, and evaluating the work of the team. By drawing out and supporting the participation and decisions of the team, the leader is in turn strengthening the abilities of each team member, so that, over time, the quality of the team's work and the ability of the team to "manage itself" improves.

Through the involvement of team members in the meaningful aspects of teamwork, team members are more apt to stay motivated, the quality level of decisions is more likely to remain high, and the implementation of decisions has a higher probability of being successful. Team leaders who lack the desire and/or skills to get people to participate run the risk of not having a team at all; they may end up working one-to-one with team members and doing all of the coordinating themselves. Worst case, they may end up doing most of the work themselves!

When a team leader takes on too much authority and responsibility, team members feel over-controlled, blocked, and under-utilized. They will generally revert to supporting only their own goals and agendas, while the overall goals of the team take a back seat. As a result, the over-controlling leader will be frustrated at the lack of support from team members and will, in many cases, become even more controlling in order to get results from the team.

On the other hand, when team leaders involve team members in all aspects of the work, from goal setting through decision making through planning and problem solving, they act as *facilitative leaders,* rather than controlling or over-directive leaders. As a facilitative leader, the team leader is more apt to get the support and buy-in of team members all along the way.

Consequences of the Controlling Leadership Style

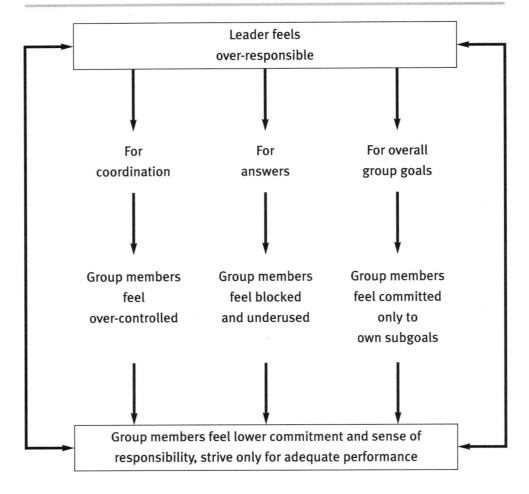

The more team members are involved, the more the leader will have a chance to let the team do its work, while the leader does his or her work. On many teams, the leader also works alongside the team members, taking the leadership role only when necessary and being a team member the rest of the time. When this happens, the facilitative team leader motivates team members to share full responsibility for the work of the team.

Activities in This Section

The activities in this section will help team leaders understand the value of getting a balance of participation from team members, identify and use basic facilitation skills, conduct a participative discussion, and learn to use tools and techniques that encourage participation.

Controlling Versus Facilitating Styles of Leadership

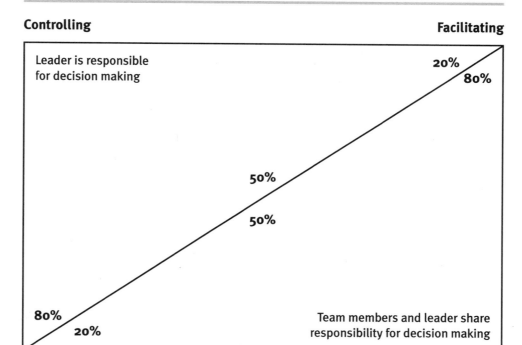

Controlling   **Facilitating**

Leader is responsible for decision making — 20% / 80%

50% / 50%

80% / 20%

Team members and leader share responsibility for decision making

**Controlling
leader's role**

- Tell
- Sell
- Direct
- Decide
- Delegate
- Solve problems
- Set goals
- Use authority to get things done

**Facilitating
leader's role**

- Listen
- Ask questions
- Direct group process
- Coach
- Teach
- Build consensus
- Share in goal setting
- Share in decision making
- Empower others to get things done

In *Activity 10, Good Team Meetings Don't Just Happen,* participants receive and trade cards with statements written on them representing elements of facilitation that are *vital* to meeting effectiveness, *harmful* to meeting effectiveness, and *reflective of style,* rather than vital or harmful. Elements are then selected and discussed to foster understanding of the effect that certain practices and behaviors have on meeting effectiveness.

Activity 11, Checklist for Planning a Team Meeting: A Brainstorming Process, involves participants in creating a checklist for planning an effective team meeting. Participants follow a classic brainstorming process and then organize the brainstormed items to create the checklist. Observers give feedback to participants on behaviors exhibited during the activity.

Activity 12, Questioning Skills for Team Leaders, teaches participants various types of questions and focuses on those that promote openness, productivity, and creativity in team meetings and in one-on-one discussions. Given a variety of situations, in a subgroup activity, participants practice coming up with appropriate questions. The large group reconvenes and participants discuss and evaluate questions formulated by the subgroups.

Activity 13, Multi-Level Listening: A Leadership Skill, addresses the need for team leaders to listen for both the content and feelings revealed in the speaker's message, while showing attentiveness and giving adequate feedback to the speaker. A Multi-Level Listening Model is introduced and discussed, and participants practice the skills of multi-level listening in triads.

Activity 14, Using Group Memory in Team Meetings, teaches participants what "group memory" is and how it contributes to effective team meetings. Participants work in subgroups to answer four questions about group memory and use flip charts to record group member input. While working in these subgroups, each participant is given the opportunity to practice recording input from his or her subgroup members.

Activity 15, Facilitation Practice for Team Leaders, is the most lengthy and comprehensive activity in the book. It is also one of the most valuable activities, because it encompasses many facilitator skills. Each participant practices leading a ten-minute facilitation and receives both written and verbal feedback from other participants and from the facilitator.

Good Team Meetings Don't Just Happen*

Purpose

- To assist participants in identifying elements of facilitation that are (1) *vital* to meeting effectiveness, (2) *harmful* to meeting effectiveness, and (3) *reflective of style,* rather than vital or harmful

- To offer the participants an opportunity to consider and discuss facilitation practices, techniques, and styles

Time

2 hours

Group Size

Designed for up to twenty people

Materials

- Flip chart and marking pens for the facilitator

- One set of fifty-two 4-inch x 6-inch index cards, each containing one of the fifty-two numbered statements on the Good Team Meetings Don't Just Happen Statement List.

- One copy of the Good Team Meetings Don't Just Happen Suggested Response Sheet for each participant, plus one copy for the facilitator

---

*Adapted from Good Workshops Don't Just Happen: Developing Facilitation Skills by Kathleen Kreis. *The 1992 Annual: Developing Human Resources,* San Francisco: Pfeiffer.

Room Setup

A room large enough for participants to move about freely and confer with one another. Movable chairs should be available as well as a table on which to place spare cards.

Steps

1. *Introduce the goals of the session and introduce the activity.* Explain that each participant will receive the same number of index cards and that each card bears a statement about facilitating a meeting. Distribute the prepared cards, leaving the extras on the table. (For example, if there are eighteen participants, each is given two cards, and the sixteen remaining cards are placed on the table.)

2. *Begin the activity.* Tell the participants to read their cards and judge whether or not each card statement describes an element that contributes to the effectiveness of a meeting. Explain that for the next few minutes the participants will be able to keep their cards or to trade, one for one, with other participants, *in order to obtain statements representing elements that contribute the most to meeting effectiveness.* A participant may choose one of the extra cards on the table, discarding another card in exchange and leaving it on the table. However, each participant must keep two cards, even if they have cards that represent behaviors that do *not* contribute to meeting effectiveness.

   After five or six minutes, announce that the participants have one more minute to complete the trading process. After another minute, call time and ask the participants to be seated.

3. *Select elements that are vital to meeting effectiveness.* Ask for volunteers to read statements from cards they are holding that represent elements *vital* to an effective meeting and explain why these elements are vital. Before the sharing begins, stipulate that after each statement is shared and explained, the listening participants will be invited to respond by agreeing or disagreeing and then stating why; subsequently, read the "suggested response" to that statement from the Good Team Meetings Don't Just Happen Suggested Response Sheet. Allow about twenty minutes for this portion of the activity.

4. *Select elements that are harmful to meeting effectiveness.* Ask volunteers who are holding cards that have not been read yet to read statements that represent elements that are *harmful* to meeting effectiveness and explain why these elements are harmful. Again, stipulate that the listening participants will be invited to agree or disagree with each assessment and that afterward the "suggested response" will be read. Allow about fifteen minutes for this portion of the activity.

5. *Select elements that reflect facilitator style.* Ask volunteers who are holding cards that have not been read yet to read them and explain why those elements *reflect facilitator style.* Ask volunteers to also state whether these elements reflect their personal preferences. Again, allow the listening participants to comment on each shared statement and read the "suggested response" for that statement. Allow about twenty minutes for this portion of the activity.

6. *Discuss remaining cards.* Lead a discussion about the cards that were left on the table after the trading process. Ask participants to classify the statements as (1) *vital* to meeting effectiveness, (2) *harmful* to meeting effectiveness, or (3) *reflective of facilitator style.* After participants have shared their opinions of each statement, read the "suggested response." Allow about fifteen minutes for this portion.

7. *Discuss conclusions.* Lead a concluding discussion based on the following questions:

   - What is the difference between a matter of style and an element that is vital to meeting effectiveness?

   - What conclusions can you draw about the elements that are vital to meeting effectiveness?

   - What conclusions can you draw about the elements that are harmful to meeting effectiveness?

   - What insights have you gained about your own style of facilitation?

   - How might you use some of the facilitation strategies that we have discussed?

   - What things might you *stop* doing to make the meetings you facilitate more effective?

8. *Wrap up the session.* Give participants each a copy of the Good Team Meetings Don't Just Happen Suggested Response Sheet and encourage them to keep it for future reference and discussion with colleagues. Review the goals for the session and ask for feedback on the session, if desired.

Variations

- Divide the participants into three subgroups, each of which is assigned the task of trading for *one* of the three categories of cards: vital, harmful, or reflective of style. After the trading period, ask each subgroup to prepare a brief presentation on its cards, citing reasons why those cards were chosen for that category. After each subgroup presents its findings, ask the other two subgroups to comment or ask questions on the material presented. Be prepared to read the response to an item from the Good Team Meetings Don't Just Happen Suggested Response Sheet if there is any confusion or disagreement.

- Introduce the activity by asking participants to discuss the best and worst meetings they have ever attended or led and the elements and critical incidents that characterized those meetings. To do this, divide the group in half and assign one half to the worst meetings they have attended and assign the other half to the best meetings they have ever attended. Ask each group to prepare a list of at least five things that made the meeting either the *worst* or the *best.*

GOOD TEAM MEETINGS DON'T JUST HAPPEN
STATEMENT LIST

1. I include both total-group and subgroup activities.

2. I offer to clarify any points that I make, asking frequently if I have been clear.

3. I post meeting objectives so everyone can see them during the meeting.

4. I keep meeting participants from getting off track and make sure they stick to the topic at hand.

5. I feel comfortable stopping at any time for questions.

6. I delay the start of a meeting until most of the participants have arrived.

7. I urge every participant to speak and offer his or her opinion.

8. I carefully plan any meetings that I lead.

9. I begin a meeting on time and end on time, no matter what.

10. I limit the number of times that a participant speaks so that no one dominates.

11. I believe in group confidentiality: what is said in the group stays in the group.

12. I make sure everyone is introduced at the beginning of a meeting, unless the participants already know one another.

13. If participants ask questions or bring up concerns that are unrelated to the topic, I record them on a flip chart for later discussion.

14. I provide frequent breaks if it is a long meeting, at least one break every one and a half hours.

15. I suggest and/or post ground rules for behavior during the meeting and ask if anyone wants to add any.

16. If participants become engaged in lengthy or loud side conversations, I call their attention back to the group.

17. I ask the group to help me come up with the next meeting's agenda before we leave the meeting.

18. I listen carefully and try to respect each participant's opinions, even if they are totally different from mine.

19. I frequently ask for feedback on how the meeting went and solicit ways future meetings could be improved.

20. When planning a meeting, I review feedback I have received from prior meetings to determine ways to make the meeting more effective.

21. I over-plan for every meeting that I facilitate—just in case.

22. I consider participant laughter to be a positive sign, indicating that participants are relaxed and that the meeting is going well.

23. I ask people to raise their hands and be recognized before they speak.

24. I make every effort to record people's inputs on flip charts and to refer back to these inputs as the meeting progresses.

25. I make every effort to draw out the ideas and opinions of the meeting participants, getting them to solve the problem and make decisions. I try to remain neutral when facilitating.

26. Sometimes, I take off my "facilitator" hat so I can contribute an idea or information that I believe may help the group.

27. I bring structure to a participative meeting by using group processes such as brainstorming, prioritizing, small group work, and so on.

28. When leading a meeting, I sometimes check with participants to see if they think the meeting is progressing well and accomplishing the objectives.

29. When possible, I plan time for people to get acquainted or socialize with one another.

30. At the beginning of a meeting, I post the objectives and the agenda for the meeting so participants know what to expect.

31. An important aspect of a meeting is for the participants to walk away feeling something was accomplished (e.g., important information received, decisions made, plans adapted, and so on).

32. Spontaneity is an important aspect of every meeting; I plan and prepare as little as possible and let the rest just happen.

33. It is important to arrange for the meeting's key points and decisions to be distributed after the meeting to all participants.

34. No participant should be forced to speak.

35. I like to keep the meeting to a definite timetable and will call time even if decisions have not been made or agreements reached.

36. If the meeting participants report to me, I try to bring in a neutral facilitator to lead important meetings whenever possible.

37. I am not concerned with the arrangement of the meeting room; I am comfortable using a large round table, classroom style setup, or other room setup.

38. I like to allow for some fun during meetings, since I believe this helps people relax and get along, especially when they are working on a difficult topic.

39. During a meeting I feel free to share my own experiences and opinions.

40. I thank participants each time they offer comments to the group.

41. If many ideas are flowing during a meeting, I ask someone else to help me record them on flip charts.

42. If someone is rambling, I interrupt and ask the speaker to sum up his or her point briefly so I can capture it on the flip chart.

43. If someone repeats an idea that was expressed earlier, I show appreciation for the comment and note that the idea has already been recorded.

44. Sometimes I sit down and let the participants carry on a discussion without me talking.

45. If a few people are dominating a discussion, I may go around the room and ask each person to share his or her opinion or ideas on the subject.

46. From time to time, I like to summarize what has been said before moving on.

47. I use someone else to record participants' inputs, because I don't want to lose eye contact with anyone who is speaking.

48. I make sure all decisions made during the meeting are agreed on and recorded for all to see.

49. When participants do not agree on a decision, I ask for consensus, meaning can everyone agree to the point that he or she will support the decision 100 percent?

50. When a problem is addressed, I allow some time up-front for people to talk about how the problem is affecting them.

51. I always provide refreshments at meetings.

52. I never talk about myself during a meeting and only share my opinions when asked.

GOOD TEAM MEETINGS DON'T JUST HAPPEN
SUGGESTED RESPONSE SHEET

1. I include both total-group and subgroup activities.
   Reflective of style. Meetings can be productive with either total-group or subgroup activities.

2. I offer to clarify any points that I make, asking frequently if I have been clear.
   Harmful. Asking to clarify points is effective; however, doing this frequently negates the positive effect of seeking to clarify.

3. I post meeting objectives so everyone can see them during the meeting.
   Vital. Posting meeting objectives helps keep everyone on track, including the facilitator. Posted objectives can easily be referred to during the meeting.

4. I keep meeting participants from getting off track and make sure they stick to the topic at hand.
   Vital. This is an important function of the meeting leader. However, it is best not to be too rigid, since an occasional veering off the topic might open up new insights on the topic at hand.

5. I feel comfortable stopping at any time for questions.
   Vital. Unanswered questions may keep participants from learning the next step of a process or skill.

6. I delay the start of a meeting until most of the participants have arrived.
   Harmful. Although some people might say this practice is a matter of style, it is important to remember that delaying in this fashion punishes participants who arrive on time and sets up a pattern for subsequent meetings to start late.

7. I urge every participant to speak and offer his or her opinion.
   Harmful. This practice may be seen as applying too much pressure. Participants should be *encouraged* to speak, but not addressed individually and *urged*.

8. I carefully plan any meetings that I lead.
   Vital. Even though skilled meeting facilitators may adapt the meeting plan when absolutely necessary, it is critical to have a well-planned structure to follow.

9. I begin a meeting on time and end on time, no matter what.
   Harmful. The phrase "no matter what" indicates inflexibility.

10. I limit the number of times that a participant speaks so that no one dominates.
    Harmful. Some might say that this approach is a style issue, but determining how many times any participant will be allowed to speak and adhering to such a limitation may squelch participation, creativity, and enthusiasm.

11. I believe in group confidentiality: what is said in the group stays in the group.
    Vital. If confidentiality is not ensured, a safe team/meeting environment cannot be created and maintained.

12. I make sure everyone is introduced at the beginning of a meeting, unless the participants already know one another.
   Vital. When meeting participants have not been introduced to one another, the spirit of working together is hindered. Also, productivity slows down because of the time it takes for participants to "figure out" who everyone is.

13. If participants ask questions or bring up concerns that are unrelated to the topic, I record them on a flip chart for later discussion.
   Vital. Recording the issue for later discussion acknowledges the contribution of the participant, while keeping the group working on the topic at hand.

14. I provide frequent breaks if it is a long meeting, at least one break every one and a half hours.
   Vital. Breaks allow participants a chance to refresh themselves, to recover from the intensity of the meeting, to become better acquainted with one another, to network, and to continue working together on an informal basis.

15. I suggest and/or post ground rules for behavior during the meeting and ask if anyone wants to add any.
   Vital: Ground rules set the standard for meeting behaviors and help make the meeting more productive. If ground rules are not followed, the meeting facilitator can refer to the posted standards and remind the group of them.

16. If participants become engaged in lengthy or loud side conversations, I call their attention back to the group.
   Reflective of style. The issue of side conversation has to be dealt with carefully. Some facilitators believe that asking participants to discontinue side conversations is inappropriate because the intervention may feel punishing to the participants. However, side conversations that are lengthy or loud may distract or annoy the participants who are trying to listen to the facilitator or to another participant who has the floor. In this case, the facilitator must exercise tact in drawing the conversing participants back to the group. A comment such as "We'd be happy to hear from everyone, but let's do it one at a time" is a tactful way to address the situation. The facilitator's goal is to *ensure group productivity and cohesiveness without creating an atmosphere that is rigid or punishing to the participants.*

17. I ask the group to help me come up with the next meeting's agenda before we leave the meeting.
   Reflective of style. Depending on the facilitator and the group, developing the agenda at the end of a meeting may work well, although this is not essential for a meeting to be effective.

18. I listen carefully and try to respect each participant's opinions, even if they are totally different from mine.
   Vital. A facilitator sets the tone for the meeting, and by listening carefully to participants' opinions helps participants feel valued, not denigrated. In addition, respectful listening encourages openness, trust, and good teamwork.

19. I frequently ask for feedback on how the meeting went and solicit ways future meetings could be improved.
   Reflective of style. The practice is a good idea but not essential to meeting effectiveness. Facilitators who regularly receive feedback, however, have the opportunity to improve future meetings as well as their skills as a facilitator.

20. When planning a meeting, I review feedback I have received from prior meetings to determine ways to make the meeting more effective.

    Reflective of style. Again, this practice is a good idea but not essential to meeting effectiveness.

21. I over-plan for every meeting that I facilitate—just in case.

    Harmful. This attitude may lead to anxiety on the part of the facilitator. A more productive attitude would be reflected in the statement, "I plan carefully for every meeting, but adapt the plan if necessary."

22. I consider participant laughter to be a positive sign, indicating that participants are relaxed and that the meeting is going well.

    Reflective of style. Laughter is not an issue related to the effectiveness of a meeting. Participants may have a positive meeting experience without laughing; on the other hand, they may be relaxed, laughing, and having a good time while being productive.

23. I ask people to raise their hands and be recognized before they speak.

    Harmful. Participants may feel that this practice is too regimented. It may stifle spontaneity, creativity, and productive interaction among the participants.

24. I make every effort to record people's inputs on flip charts and to refer back to these inputs as the meeting progresses.

    Vital. Making people's inputs visible for all to see is an important way to keep the meeting progressing and to ensure that everyone's ideas are considered.

25. I make every effort to draw out the ideas and opinions of the meeting participants, getting them to solve the problem and make decisions. I try to remain neutral when facilitating.

    Vital. This is the very essence of facilitating and is critical to effective teamwork.

26. Sometimes, I take off my "facilitator" hat so I can contribute an idea or information that I believe may help the group.

    Reflective of style. A productive meeting can take place with or without input on the part of the facilitator. Some participants expect the facilitator to share information, whereas others prefer that the facilitator remain neutral. It is important, though, that personal opinions be presented as just that—opinions. Presenting them as "truth" undermines the facilitator's credibility.

27. I bring structure to a participative meeting by using group processes such as brainstorming, prioritizing, small group work, and so on.

    Vital. Simply getting people involved is not enough. There must be structure to the participation for the meeting to proceed successfully.

28. When leading a meeting, I sometimes check with participants to see if they think the meeting is progressing well and accomplishing the objectives.

    Reflective of style. This is a good practice in certain instances. It should be used minimally, since overuse would slow meeting progress and undermine the credibility of the facilitator.

29. When possible, I plan time for people to get acquainted or socialize with one another.

    Reflective of style. Depending on the subject and purpose of the meeting, it may be valuable to plan in time for people to socialize with one another. However, meetings can be effective without social time.

30. At the beginning of a meeting, I post the objectives and the agenda for the meeting so participants know what to expect.

    Vital. It is important to be clear up-front about the purpose and flow of the meeting so participants can focus on what must be done. This promotes trust, commitment, and participation. On the other hand, springing surprises on the participants hinders a productive meeting environment and creates trust issues between the facilitator and the participants.

31. An important aspect of a meeting is for the participants to walk away feeling something was accomplished (e.g., important information received, decisions made, plans adapted, and so on).

    Vital. When participants feel they have contributed to a meeting that accomplished what it set out to accomplish, they are more confident about and committed to the work of the team.

32. Spontaneity is an important aspect of every meeting; I plan and prepare as little as possible and let the rest just happen.

    Harmful. Flexibility is important, and spontaneity is valuable at certain points in a meeting, but failing to plan and prepare carefully may lead to disaster.

33. It is important to arrange for the meeting's key points and decisions to be distributed after the meeting to all participants.

    Vital. Participants need to see their decisions and plans in writing so they will be clear and move in the agreed-on direction.

34. No participant should be forced to speak.

    Vital. Coercion undermines the freedom of individuals to participate. It also places too much control in the hands of the facilitator.

35. I like to keep the meeting to a definite timetable and will call time even if decisions have not been made or agreements reached.

    Harmful. Even though it can be an effective facilitation technique to call time during certain activities, trying to keep to a definite timetable may hinder productivity.

36. If the meeting participants report to me, I try to bring in a neutral facilitator to lead important meetings whenever possible.

    Reflective of style. Bringing in an outside, neutral facilitator can be a good practice if there is time and resources to do so. However, team leaders and managers can learn to use facilitation skills to lead their meetings.

37. I am not concerned with the arrangement of the meeting room; I am comfortable using a large round table, classroom style setup, or other room setup.

    Harmful. The setup of the room is an important part of the meeting environment and affects the ability of the participants to communicate and work well together.

38. I like to allow for some fun during meetings, since I believe this helps people relax and get along, especially when they are working on a difficult topic.

    Reflective of style. Planned and spontaneous fun can help participants relax during an intense meeting, although it is not essential to an effective meeting.

25 Activities for Developing Team Leaders. Copyright © 2005 by John Wiley & Sons, Inc. Reproduced by permission of Pfeiffer, an Imprint of Wiley. www.pfeiffer.com

39. During a meeting I feel free to share my own experiences and opinions.
   Harmful. The meeting facilitator may share experiences or opinions once or twice without affecting the participation of others in the meeting, but doing this too often shuts down the participants and hurts facilitator credibility.

40. I thank participants each time they offer comments to the group.
   Harmful. Thanking participants occasionally helps sets the tone of appreciation, but thanking participants for every comment is detrimental to group progress and makes the facilitator appear "robotic" or insincere.

41. If many ideas are flowing during a meeting, I ask someone else to help me record them on flip charts.
   Reflective of style. Although this is an effective technique, it is not essential and not always practical.

42. If someone is rambling, I interrupt and tactfully ask the speaker to sum up his or her point briefly so I can capture it on the flip chart.
   Vital. This is a facilitator skill that helps keep the meeting moving and encourages people to state their points as succinctly as possible.

43. If someone repeats an idea that was expressed earlier, I show appreciation for the comment and note that the idea has already been recorded.
   Vital. This encourages people to listen carefully to one another and to avoid being redundant.

44. Sometimes I sit down and let the participants carry on a discussion without me talking.
   Reflective of style. Although not essential to a productive meeting, this can be an effective way to allow participants to work together.

45. If a few people are dominating a discussion, I use various techniques to get other people to share their opinions or ideas on the subject.
   Vital. When a meeting or discussion is dominated by a few people, other participants are excluded and the meeting is not truly a participative one.

46. From time to time, I like to summarize what has been said before moving on.
   Vital. Summarizing gives participants time to digest what has been said or accomplished before moving on to the next meeting task.

47. I use someone else to record participants' inputs because I don't want to lose eye contact with anyone who is speaking.
   Reflective of style. Some facilitators are comfortable writing while listening. Others prefer a different approach. Both can be effective in a meeting.

48. I make sure all decisions made during the meeting are agreed on and recorded for all to see.
   Vital. Posting decisions clarifies them, helps people remember what was decided, and avoids misunderstandings about what was actually decided.

49. When participants do not agree on a decision, I ask for consensus, meaning can everyone agree to the point that he or she will support the decision 100 percent?
   Vital. Frequently, participants disagree on what is the best decision. Reaching consensus means people agree to support a decision so the team can move forward.

50. When a problem is addressed, I allow some time up-front for people to talk about how the problem is affecting them.
Reflective of style. It is often helpful to let people air their concerns and feelings about a particular problem, but it may not be essential or productive in all cases.

51. I always provide refreshments at meetings.
Reflective of style. Meetings can be effective with or without refreshments.

52. I never talk about myself during a meeting and only share my opinions when asked.
Harmful. Being too "secretive" or reserved may distance the facilitator from the group, breed distrust, or set the tone for others to be the same. Facilitators should minimize sharing their personal information or opinions in order to focus on the task of facilitating *others* to participate.

Checklist for Planning a Team Meeting: A Brainstorming Process

Purpose

- To develop a checklist for planning an effective team meeting
- To experience a brainstorming activity
- To accomplish three steps using material from the brainstorming activity: *clarify* the ideas, *discuss* the ideas, and *organize* the ideas
- To identify effective and ineffective team behaviors during an organizing activity

Time

1 1/2 to 2 hours

Group Size

Designed for ten to fifteen people

Materials

- Flip chart and marking pens for the facilitator
- Pen/pencil and paper for each participant
- One Brainstorming Guidelines sheet for each participant
- One Brainstorming Observer Sheet for each participant

Room Setup

U-shape (see diagram on page 22)

Steps

1. *Explain the purpose of the session.* Distribute paper and a pen or pencil to each participant and introduce the activity by asking participants to quickly write down their answers to the following question:

   > You are going to hold an important team meeting for your team. The team members will be traveling from various states, and it is the first time all of the team members have been together. What is the first thing you would do to begin preparing for the meeting?

   Allow participants about one minute to write down their answers. Go around the room and ask each person to introduce him- or herself and read his or her answer. After all the answers have been read, comment on either the similarity or differences of the answers. If answers were quite different, explain that it is not always clear what needs to be done to plan an effective meeting. Mention that because we are all often short of time, meetings are planned in a flurry of other activities. Suggest that, because much of the success of a meeting depends on how it is set up, it might be helpful for team leaders to have a generic checklist of pre-meeting activities they can refer to when planning a meeting.

   Tell the participants that when they leave this session, they will have a checklist of pre-meeting activities for a meeting similar to the situation explained above—meetings that bring together team members from various sites. Explain that not all meetings require extensive planning, that team meetings may be called on the spur of the moment. However, in most instances, a team leader can be more efficient using a checklist, which eliminates the need to make a to-do list up for every meeting.

2. *Begin the brainstorming activity.* Ask participants to write as many things as they can think of that must be done before a team meeting. Ask them *not* to think about *who* should do these things but simply all the things that must be done. Tell them that they should not judge their ideas and that *quantity* is more important than quality. Allow about ten minutes for this assignment.

3. *Collect ideas.* Using two recorders and two flip charts, go around the room and ask participants to state one of their ideas at a time, listening to others so that ideas are not repeated. *Note:* Select and coach the recorders ahead of time (before the session begins, if possible). Tell them to write large and use a bullet point to denote each new idea. Instruct them to ask for an idea to be repeated, if necessary, and to shorten the comments without changing any of the meanings. Ask each recorder to write every other idea, so that all ideas are recorded as quickly as possible.

Do not allow discussion or questions about the ideas at this time; simply record the ideas. Move quickly around the room. Tell participants to write new ideas down as they think of them, to piggyback on others' ideas, and to allow other ideas to stimulate new ideas. When a participant runs out of ideas, he or she should say, "Pass." Continue to go around the room and let participants who passed on an earlier round add new ideas as they think of them.

Once the flow of ideas dies down, ask if anyone has any other ideas. Make sure the recorders get all ideas.

4. *Stop the brainstorming session.* Explain to the participants that they have just experienced the first stage of brainstorming—the "dreaming up" and quick recording of everyone's ideas, along with the creation of new ideas as ideas are recorded. Explain that the time for individuals to first think on their own is an important step in the process, one that is frequently overlooked.

5. *Distribute copies of the handout.* Point out to participants that they have just completed the first section of the handout and briefly review the importance of the guidelines. Tell the participants that they will be working through the second process now.

6. *Clarifying the meaning of the ideas.* Tell the participants that they will now move into the first of three phases of work following a brainstorming session: (1) *clarify* the ideas, so that everyone understands what each idea means; (2) *discuss* the merits of the ideas and eliminate any that are not workable; and (3) *organize* the ideas for further use. Have the recorders post the flip charts around the room. Ask participants to review the lists and look for any statements they do not understand or would like further clarification of. Do not allow evaluation of the ideas at this time—only *clarification* of what the contributor of the idea meant. It is important to consider and understand

each idea before evaluating it. If necessary, the recorders should change the wording of an idea for clarity.

7. *Discuss the merits of the ideas.* Ask participants to select any items they would like to discuss or eliminate from the list. If any items are eliminated, make sure everyone agrees. If only some think the item should be eliminated, mark that item with an asterisk and leave it on the list. Tell the group that it is experiencing the *second* phase after brainstorming, which is the *discussion* phase. Mention that, during this phase, it can be helpful to make sure the merits of all ideas have been acknowledged before eliminating any items. Identifying the merits of an idea can stimulate creative thinking and highlight ideas that are important.

8. *Work in subgroups to organize the material.* Tell the group that it is moving into the *third* phase after brainstorming, the *organizing* phase. Divide the group into two subgroups. Have one subgroup organize all the items into a chronological flow, showing the order of when the items should be accomplished when planning a meeting. Encourage the group to come to agreement on the chronological flow. Distribute a Brainstorming Observer Sheet to each member of the second subgroup and have the second subgroup observe the work of the first subgroup and complete the Brainstorming Observer Sheet. After about twenty minutes, or when the first subgroup is about 50 percent done with the assignment, stop the activity and have the second subgroup continue the work. Distribute a Brainstorming Observer Sheet to each member of the first subgroup. Members of the first subgroup now become the observers. Allow about twenty minutes for the second subgroup to finish organizing the brainstormed list.

9. *Debrief the activity.* When the second subgroup is finished, ask the participants to return to their seats for a discussion of the activity. First, ask the two subgroups what they think of their work. Is this a checklist they can really use? If yes, state why. If not, state why. If it is not usable, what must be done to make it usable? Next, ask the first subgroup to work on the list what went well in the time it worked together. What could have been done differently to improve the group's productivity and product? Ask the second subgroup the same questions about how it worked together on the brainstormed list. (*Do not allow observers to comment on their observations at this time. All participants are to comment on their experience working in a team to organize the list.*)

Finally, ask observers of the first subgroup to comment on how the group worked together, responding to the questions on the Brainstorming Observer Sheet. Next, ask the observers of the second subgroup to comment on how the group worked together, responding to the questions from the Brainstorming Observer Sheet.

10. *Summarize the learning.* Ask participants to comment on the following questions to summarize the brainstorming and organizing activities:

    - What did you learn about brainstorming from today's session?

    - What was effective about the brainstorming process as it was experienced today?

    - What would have improved the brainstorming process as it was experienced today?

    - What did the subgroups do during the organizing activity that was particularly effective as a team?

    - What could the subgroups have done *differently* during the organizing activity to work more effectively as a team?

    - How do you feel about the list you came up with in the subgroups? What do you want to do with the list?

11. *Wrap up the session.* Encourage someone in the group to transcribe the list and distribute it to all the participants. If the list is not finished, ask if someone (or a small group of people) will finish it and route it to everyone. Ask if a small subgroup would like to get together after the session and create a checklist for team meetings when team members are all located at the same site. If so, agree on a time for the checklist to be completed and distributed to the participants. Ask for feedback on the session, if desired (see "Managing the Group Training Session: Tips for Trainers" in the Introduction, page 11), and adjourn.

BRAINSTORMING GUIDELINES

The purpose of brainstorming is to generate as many ideas as possible to achieve the goal, answer the question, address the problem, etc.

Follow these guidelines:

1. All ideas are OK. Do not censor your ideas.

2. Aim for quantity, not quality.

3. "Wild" ideas are OK. They may generate usable ideas.

4. Do not discuss or evaluate ideas at this time.

5. Build on others' ideas if possible.

6. "Pass" if you run out of ideas.

After Brainstorming, Then What?

After brainstorming, follow the process below to clarify, discuss, and organize the ideas:

1. *Clarify the ideas.* Make sure everyone understands what each idea means. (Do not evaluate the ideas; just make sure they are clear.)

2. *Discuss the ideas.* Select ideas that merit consideration or further discussion. Allow people to put forth both the advantages and disadvantages of an idea. Discuss whether the idea relates to the goal at hand.

3. *Organize the ideas.* If necessary or helpful, organize the ideas into categories, topics, etc.

This may complete the process, or further work may be called for, such as prioritizing ideas, selecting the best ideas, and/or eliminating ideas.

BRAINSTORMING OBSERVER SHEET

Instructions: Answer the questions below as you observe your subgroup organizing the ideas.

1. Was there a balance of participation? If so, how was this achieved?

2. Did participants listen well to one another?

3. How did the work proceed (did the group organize itself, was there a group leader, etc.)?

4. How were differences resolved?

5. What was particularly effective about the way the group worked together?

6. What could have been done differently to improve the group's teamwork?

Questioning Skills for Team Leaders

Purpose

- To develop facility in recognizing and using various types of questions to promote openness, productivity, and creativity in team meetings and in one-on-one discussions

Time

1 1/2 to 2 hours

Group Size

Designed for ten to sixteen people

Materials

- Flip chart and marking pens for the facilitator
- Prepared flip chart page (see Step 2)
- Flip chart paper, marking pens, and masking tape for each subgroup
- One Questioning Skills Types of Questions handout per person
- One Questioning Skills Situation Sheet per person

Room Setup

U-shape (see diagram on page 22)

Steps

1. *Introduce the goals of the session.* Explain that the ability to ask questions is a critical skill for team leaders and facilitators. Point out that it is a skill to craft a question and that asking a question sincerely is an important step in becoming a listening leader as well as an effective facilitator. Announce that during this session, participants will learn how to recognize and craft different types of questions and to determine when to use certain types of questions.

2. *Lead a demonstration of the effects questions have on listeners.* Ask the questions listed below. After each question, pause and ask the participants to think about their response. Then ask them to indicate with a show of hands whether their response would have been (1) one or two words, (2) open and explanatory, (3) creative, (4) guarded, (5) sarcastic, (6) other. (Prepare a flip chart ahead of time with these six responses listed.)

   Questions to ask:

   a. Did you have time for breakfast this morning?

   b. Were you on time to work today?

   c. What do you think of the weather we are having?

   d. Where do you like to go for vacations?

   e. What is your opinion of the traffic in many of today's cities?

   f. Are you good at saving money?

   g. What challenges do you face in investing for your future?

   h. What do you love about your job?

   i. What can people do to improve their overall health?

   j. What type of person would you like to work with on a team?

   Go quickly through the questions and don't discuss reactions. After all questions have been asked and reactions indicated, ask participants *why* they reacted in different ways to the questions. List responses on a flip chart. Post the chart.

3. *Ask participants to think of themselves as team leaders.* Why is it important for team leaders to ask questions of their team members? List responses on a flip chart. Don't try to get an exhaustive list; just get everyone thinking about the reasons team leaders need to ask questions.

4. *Explain the importance of questioning skills for team leaders.* Explain that questions are an effective way to start a productive discussion, to clarify understanding, and to come to closure—whether in a one-on-one meeting or in a group meeting. Team leaders and facilitators learn to use questions productively, not to manipulate a person or group, but to help the communication or meeting proceed in a productive fashion. *Developing good questioning skills helps team leaders get productivity from their teams.* Just as the participants reacted in different ways to the different types of questions above, so will team members react differently to questions in a one-on-one or group discussion.

5. *Explain the types of questions.* Distribute the Questioning Skills Types of Questions handout and explain each type of question. Go back over the list of ten questions above, this time asking the participants to identify whether each question is a closed question or an open question. (*Note to trainer:* Questions c, e, g, i, and j are Open questions; questions a, b, and f are Closed questions; questions d and h are potentially open or closed, depending on the listener's response. Both questions d and h could be reworded to be more open. Question d could be reworded to ask, "What, in your opinion, makes a really good vacation?" Question h could be reworded to ask, "What do you like most and least about your job?")

6. *Discuss hidden agendas.* Ask if any of the ten questions seem to have a "hidden agenda." Why do they think this? Discuss the concept of hidden agendas in questions so there is mutual understanding and agreement. (See the Types of Questions handout for reference). Point out that it is sometimes difficult to tell whether there is a hidden agenda to a question; this depends on the context in which the question appears, the point of view of the listener, and the intent of the questioner. Basically, team leaders should try to pose open and closed questions with a desire to gain insight and increase productivity, not to trick the listener or to hide their own agendas in a question. Ask the participants if they can think of any "hidden agenda" questions they have heard recently that they can share with the group.

7. *Introduce the next exercise.* Explain that participants are going to create some of their own open, closed, and hidden agenda questions for several situations. Divide the group into subgroups of three to four people each and distribute a Questioning Skills Situation Sheet to each participant. Tell the subgroups that they will all be responding to all the items on the sheet and that they should follow the instructions on the Questioning Skills Situation Sheet. Ask each subgroup to appoint a recorder to record the questions the subgroup creates. Allow about thirty minutes for the subgroups to work. Give each subgroup flip chart paper, pens, and masking tape and have them gather in various areas of the room. Tell them to begin.

8. *Report on the activity.* Bring the total group back together. Read each situation aloud and have each subgroup read its question(s) for that situation. After each question is read, ask the group, "What kind of question is that (open, closed, or hidden agenda)?" After the questions for each situation have been read, ask:

   - Do all of the questions fit the situation?

   - If not, why not?

   - Are there questions that might need to be reformulated? If so, which ones?

   Go through all of the situations this way.

9. *Wrap up the session.* Review the purpose of the session. Ask the participants what they have learned about asking questions that will help them in leading teams. Go around the room to hear from each participant. Ask for feedback on the session (see "Managing the Group Training Session: Tips for Trainers" in the Introduction, page 11) and adjourn.

QUESTIONING SKILLS TYPES OF QUESTIONS

Open Questions (Also Called Open-Ended Questions)

This type of question prompts the listener to respond with more than a few words. Open questions encourage participants to supply ideas, opinions, reactions, or information. Open questions cannot be answered with a simple "Yes" or "No" or by supplying a fact. Use open-ended questions when you want people to think and participate, especially to generate a lot of ideas or data. An open-ended question can be very effective to explore a subject more deeply or to help group members be more honest with one another. Depending on how and when they are used, well-worded, open questions promote creativity, stimulate broad and/or in-depth discussion, and draw out a variety of ideas and opinions. Sincere, open questions have the effect of building rapport with people, encouraging involvement and participation, and showing confidence in the opinions and ideas of others.

Open questions usually begin with "What," "How," "Who," or "Why." Although they do not technically ask a question, the words, "Tell me. . ." have the same effect as an open question and can be used effectively with individuals or groups.

Examples of Open Questions

- What is your reaction to that?
- How can this process be improved?
- What alternatives do we have?
- What suggestions do you have for. . . ?
- How does that relate to our goal of. . . ?
- What do others in the group think?
- Tell me more about. . . .

Closed Questions (Also Called Closed-Ended Questions)

Closed questions prompt the listener to respond with a simple "Yes," "No," or a fact. They have the effect of finding out facts or guiding the individual or group to closure on a topic. In one-on-one communication and in meetings, they are used to propel the process forward, to move on to the next step, to wrap up a discussion, to obtain more specific information, or to direct people to reach consensus.

Use caution when asking closed questions, as too many closed-ended questions can have the effect of stifling or frustrating an individual or group. If not worded carefully, they can put someone on the defensive or create a negative atmosphere. A team leader or facilitator who uses too many closed-ended questions may actually steer the group (whether consciously or unconsciously) in the direction he or she wants it to go, or so it may appear to group members. This can have a controlling rather than a facilitating effect. When used wisely and appropriately, closed questions need not be controlling, but can have a powerful and productive effect on group decision making and productivity.

Examples of Closed Questions

- Does anyone have any other points to make before we move on?
- Has this type of problem ever occurred before?
- Is everyone ready, then, to move on to the next step in the process?

"Hidden Agenda" Questions

These are either open or closed questions that seem to mask a hidden agenda, depending on the way they are asked or the context in which they occur. When a person asks a hidden agenda question, he or she is not being open and honest about what he or she wishes to find out. Or he or she is asking one question to get at something else. For example, the question "Are you good at saving money?" might be suspected of having a hidden agenda because of the way it is asked. The listener might think the questioner is going to be critical or will use the answer to manipulate the listener. A more open way to ask the question would be, "How do you feel about saving money?" This is less apt to put the listener on the defensive and give him or her plenty of room to respond without feeling criticized or attacked. Hidden agenda questions should be avoided since they can undermine trust and make open communication difficult.

Both open and closed questions can turn into hidden agenda questions, depending on when, how, and in what tone of voice the question is asked. Hidden agendas creep in when the leader or facilitator fails to remain neutral and tries to steer the group in a certain direction. Team leaders and facilitators can use open and closed questions effectively if they remain neutral and are open-minded and sincere about wanting an honest response.

QUESTIONING SKILLS SITUATION SHEET

Instructions: Assign someone to be the recorder for your group. The recorder can participate in the activity as well.

For each situation below, create an appropriate *open* or *closed* question. Write the number of the situation on flip-chart paper followed by the question your subgroup selects. In some of the situations, you will be asked to create a "hidden agenda" question in addition to the most appropriate question. Write out the "hidden agenda" question your group selects.

Remember: you are learning to recognize hidden agenda questions so that you will *avoid* using them, since they are not productive in communication and in team meetings.

Situation 1

Team members have been discussing a recurring problem related to work flow. Some tasks are being done more than once, and some are falling through the cracks and not being done at all. Ask a question to focus the team on solving the problem.

Question:

Situation 2

You have posted meeting objectives and an agenda that you would like to accomplish at today's team meeting. Ask a question to see if team members agree to work on these objectives.

Question:

Situation 3

A team member has briefly mentioned a concern that no one has brought up before. She has made only a brief comment, and you would like to know about the specifics of her concern. Ask a question to encourage her to share more information.

Question:

Situation 4

Team members have veered off the subject several times during the meeting to talk about a concern that has nothing to do with the meeting's objectives. Ask a question to determine how serious this concern is and to help you decide whether to postpone the meeting's objectives and pursue the team members' concern.

Question:

Situation 5

Several of the team's norms (standards of operating) are being violated by some of the team members, such as being on time to meetings, showing respect for everyone's ideas, and supporting team decisions 100 percent. You would like the team to discuss this during the meeting you have called. (1) Ask a question to open up the conversation and to encourage team members to evaluate how well the team is supporting its stated norms. (2) Ask a hidden agenda question.

Question 1:

Question 2:

Situation 6

Your team is beginning a new project. Ask a question to focus the team on coming up with the goals for the project.

Question:

Situation 7

Your team has listed fourteen problems it is facing as a team. You would like the team members to move on and identify which problems to focus on first. (1) Ask a question to move the team forward. (2) Ask a hidden agenda question.

Question 1:

Question 2:

Situation 8

Everyone on the team seems to agree to the suggestions being made. Ask a question to find out if anyone is holding back his or her real thoughts or feelings.

Question:

Situation 9

A team member has made a suggestion that has been ignored by his or her teammates. Ask a question to get other team members to think about and review the suggestion.

Question:

Situation 10

Attendance at team meetings has not been good for the last two team meetings. Since this seriously slows the team's progress, you are concerned. Come up with (1) a question to ask the team members present at the current meeting and (2) a similar or different question to ask those who are absent from this meeting.

Question 1:

Question 2:

Multi-Level Listening:
A Leadership Skill

Purpose

- To identify barriers to effective listening
- To identify effective listening behaviors
- To understand the concept and importance of multi-level listening
- To develop skills in multi-level listening
- To select personal goals to improve listening skills

Time

2 to 2 1/2 hours

Group Size

Designed for nine to eighteen people

Materials

- Two easels, flip chart paper, marking pens, and masking tape for the facilitator
- Prizes for winning team (something team members can share such as a box of candy, pens, pencils, bookmarks, etc.) Have enough prizes for both teams just in case there is a tie.

- A prepared flip chart page of the Multi-Level Listening Model (see Multi-Level Listening Skills handout)

- One Multi-Level Listening Skills Practice sheet, cut into individual pieces of paper and placed in a container for drawing out one by one

- One Multi-Level Listening Skills handout per participant

- One Multi-Level Listening Skills Practice Instructions sheet per participant

- One Multi-Level Listening Skills Practice Observer Sheet per participant, plus a few extra

- Pens or pencils for participants

Room Setup

A room large enough for participants to move about freely and confer with one another. Movable chairs should be available, as well as plenty of wall space for posting flip charts.

Steps

1. *Introduce the goals of the session and lead a discussion.* Open the session with a discussion of the importance of listening for team leaders. Using two flip-chart sheets at the front of the room, title one "Listens Well" and the other "Doesn't Listen Well." Ask participants to think of a colleague, team leader, boss, teacher, doctor, or other person they have known who *listened well.* Ask, "What were some of your personal reactions, behaviors, and/or feelings as a result of that person's effective listening?" List their responses on the chart titled "Listens Well."

   After a few minutes, switch the topic and ask the participants to think of a colleague, team leader, boss, teacher, doctor, or other person they have known who *did not listen well.* Ask, "What were some of your personal reactions, behaviors, and/or feelings as a result of that person's ineffective listening?" List their responses on the chart titled "Doesn't Listen Well." After a few minutes, ask participants to look at the two sets of responses and summarize what they see. Ask them what are probably the worst outcomes for them if someone doesn't listen well. Put an asterisk by those items.

2. *Summarize.* Summarize the discussion by asking participants if they agree that their personal performance, their trust level, and their sense of satisfaction are generally improved when working or dealing with someone who listens well. Ask, "Why is it particularly important for team leaders to listen effectively?" List their responses on a chart titled "Why Team Leaders Need to Listen Effectively."

3. *Introduce team activity.* Divide the group into two teams. Tell the teams they are going to be creating two different lists. The team with the most items on its list after time is called will win a prize. Place two easels at opposite ends of the room. Assign each team a number (Team 1 and Team 2). Announce that Team 1 will be listing Barriers to Effective Listening and that Team 2 will be listing Effective Listening Behaviors. Tell the teams that they will be given ten minutes to complete their respective lists. When time is called they can finish only the item that is being written at the time. The team with the greatest number of items listed wins a prize.

4. *Conduct the team activity.* Call time after ten minutes. Have each team count its number of items. Have a spokesperson from each team read his or her team's list out loud for the entire group. Award a prize to the team with the greatest number of items. (Be prepared to award two team prizes if there is a tie.) Thank the teams and leave the lists posted in the room.

5. *Present the Multi-Level Listening Model.* Post a prepared flip chart containing the Multi-Level Listening Model from the Multi-Level Listening Skills handout. (Post only the model, not the other information or techniques.) Briefly explain what each part of the model means and why it is important for team leaders. (*Do not distribute copies of the handout to the participants.*)

   As you explain the model, ask participants to come up with techniques to support each of the four areas of the model. Use the questions below and record responses on the flip charts. Post the flip-chart sheets as you go along. Suggest that participants refer back to their lists and find examples that support the model.

   • What are some ways we as listeners can comprehend the *content* or message of the speaker? (List responses on a chart titled Listen for Content.)

   • What are some ways we as listeners can "hear" the *feelings* or sense the motivation of the speaker? Where do we get our clues as to the emotional level of the speaker's words? (List responses on a chart titled Listen for Feelings.)

- What are some ways we as listeners can show *attentiveness* to the speaker? How can we keep focused and attentive even though there may be potential distractions? (List responses on a chart titled Listen with Attentiveness.)

- What are some ways we as listeners can give *feedback* to the speaker to show we have truly heard him or her and that we understand and/or have empathy? (List responses on a chart titled Listen with Feedback.)

6. *Introduce the skill practice.* Distribute one copy of the Multi-Level Listening Skills handout to each participant and explain that examples of the various listening skills are listed. Give them a few minutes to read over the handout and ask questions.

   Announce that participants are going to practice using and observing effective listening techniques based on the Multi-Level Listening Model. First, ask each participant to select two skills he or she would like to practice and improve, one each from two of the four areas of the model. For example, a participant might select "eye contact" (to practice and improve listening for attentiveness) and "asking open questions" (to improve listening for content).

7. *Give instructions to triads.* Divide the group into subgroups of three people each. Explain that during the practice activity, each person will be the speaker once, the listener once, and the observer once. Distribute the Multi-Level Listening Skills Practice Instructions and suggest that participants follow along as you explain the process they will be using.

8. *Start the listening practice.* Once you have clarified the instructions as necessary, tell the triads to find separate areas of the room for the listening practice and hand out Multi-Level Listening Skills Practice Observer Sheets and pens or pencils. Conduct the first round. Walk around the room to make sure all triads are proceeding correctly. Repeat the listening practice round three or more times so all participants have a chance to be the listener at least once. Encourage groups to continue practicing during each round, even if everyone has had one chance to be the listener.

9. *Debrief the listening practice activity.* After all the rounds have been completed, bring the entire group back together and ask participants the following questions:

   - What was it like to be the *speaker* during the practice activity?
   - What was it like to be the *observer*?

- What was it like to be the *listener*?
- What listening skills proved to be the most challenging?
- What did you learn about listening from this practice activity?

10. *Wrap up the session.* Return to the goals and remind participants that they should use the Multi-Level Listening Skills handout to improve their listening skills. Summarize what you heard were the main insights gained from this activity. Ask for feedback on the session (see "Managing the Group Training Session: Tips for Trainers" in the Introduction, page 11) and adjourn.

MULTI-LEVEL LISTENING SKILLS

> ## Multi-Level Listening Model
>
> **Listen *for***
> - Content
> - Feelings
>
> **Listen *with***
> - Attentiveness
> - Feedback

Effective listening requires concentration by the listener on several levels. The listener actually plays an important role in what and how the speaker communicates. If the listener is inattentive, interrupts, misinterprets, or gives negative or inadequate feedback to the speaker, the quality and possibly even the content of the speaker's words will be affected. To encourage the speaker and give him or her the best possible environment in which to communicate, the listener should listen on several levels.

The listener must comprehend the *content* of the message he or she is hearing, while at the same time ascertaining the *feelings* or motivations of the speaker. To encourage the speaker to be open and accurate in communication, the listener needs to show *attentiveness* with good eye contact and appropriate body language and avoid interrupting the speaker or allowing distractions to draw attention away from the speaker. An effective listener gives clues and *feedback* to the speaker that assure the speaker that he or she is being understood.

Multi-Level Listening Techniques

Techniques to Listen for Content

- Repeat words and phrases in your mind as the speaker speaks.
- Summarize in your mind what the speaker is saying.
- Remember points the speaker is making to support his or her ideas.
- Avoid thinking of what you are going to say next.
- Try to imagine visually what the speaker is saying (create images in your mind).
- If confused, tell the speaker you are confused, explain what you think you have heard so far, and ask if this is correct.
- Probe for more information (Ask questions such as, "What then?" "What else happened?" "Are there other things I should know?").
- Clarify your understanding by paraphrasing back what the speaker has said.
- Avoid interrupting.

Techniques to Listen for Feelings

- Notice speaker's tone of voice, voice inflections.
- Note body language and facial expressions that may be clues to feelings.

- Note choices of words that may indicate how the speaker feels.
- Ask how the speaker feels about what he or she is saying.

Techniques to Listen with Attentiveness

- Use ways listed above to listen for content.
- Use ways listed above to listen for feelings.
- Maintain good eye contact.
- Show interest with body language (head nods, leaning forward, etc.).
- Ask pertinent and appropriate questions (but don't over-question).
- Tell the speaker what you are thinking or feeling about what he or she has said.
- Give responses that indicate you're following what the speaker is saying ("um," "I see," etc.).
- Don't stray from the speaker's subject or take over the conversation.

Techniques to Listen with Feedback

- Show empathy for what the speaker has said or is feeling.
- Check for understanding if you are confused.
- Summarize key points the speaker has made.
- Respond directly to something the speaker says.

MULTI-LEVEL LISTENING SKILLS PRACTICE TOPICS

Note to instructor: Copy this sheet and cut it into individual topics for drawing. There are nine examples. Copy this sheet more than once so you have plenty of topic sheets for the size group you are training.

Speaker: Tell the listener about what it's like raising a family or what it's like to be a member of a family. ("Family" can be whatever you define to be family. If you have an unconventional definition of "family," let the listener know.)

Speaker: Tell the listener about your favorite hobby or pastime, how you got into the hobby/pastime, and what you find beneficial about it. Also, tell the listener some of the disadvantages of your hobby/pastime, if there are any.

Speaker: Talk about the advantages and disadvantages of living where you currently live. Tell the listener where you would live if you could, why you would live there, and what you would probably miss about your current "home" if you left.

Speaker: Tell the listener about trends that are evident in our society today. Try to cover both positive and negative trends and why you see them as positive or negative.

Speaker: Name at least two other "careers" you might have pursued or would like to pursue. Explain why you are drawn to these careers and why you chose the one you are currently in over the others.

Speaker: Talk about having a "life purpose." What does the term "life purpose" mean to you? Do you think it is possible to have one central purpose in life? Why or why not? If you have ever gone through an exercise to determine your life purpose, tell about the process (you do not need to share your life purpose, if you have one, unless you want to).

Speaker: Tell the listener two or three things you value highly in life and why. For each of the values you mention, tell about behaviors that you think support this value. In other words, if someone has this value, how does he or she act in real life? How did you come to highly value these things you mentioned?

Speaker: Tell the listener about balancing life and work, or work and family. What do you find particularly challenging about balancing work and family/personal life? What strategies or techniques do you find useful for achieving balance? What remains unbalanced?

Speaker: Tell the listener what makes you feel appreciated and of value to the organization you work for. Be as specific as you can be. Next, tell the listener what makes you feel unappreciated or under-utilized. If you could change your organization, what one or two things would you change to make it a more fulfilling place for you to work?

25 Activities for Developing Team Leaders. Copyright © 2005 by John Wiley & Sons, Inc. Reproduced by permission of Pfeiffer, an Imprint of Wiley. www.pfeiffer.com

MULTI-LEVEL LISTENING SKILLS
PRACTICE INSTRUCTIONS

Instructions: Each person will be the speaker once, the listener once, and the observer once. Follow the process outlined below:

1. The listener announces to the speaker and observer what skills he or she has selected to practice.

2. The speaker draws a topic from the "hat" at the front of the room.

3. The speaker begins speaking on that topic and tries to make sure the listener fully understands what he or she is saying. The speaker pauses now and then to allow the listener to respond.

4. The observer takes notes on the Observer Sheet.

5. Time is called, and the triad debriefs the activity, as follows:

   - The speaker tells the listener what was effective and what would have been more effective about the listener's techniques.

   - The observer gives feedback to the listener, based on notes taken on the Observer Sheet.

   - The listener tells the speaker and observer how he or she felt during the activity, what went well, what was difficult, and what he or she could do next time to be a better listener.

MULTI-LEVEL LISTENING SKILLS
PRACTICE OBSERVER SHEET

Instructions: Put a checkmark beside any of the skills or techniques the listener uses. Make a note if there were techniques the listener could have used but did not. Notice in what area the listener was most effective (listening for *content,* listening for *feelings,* listening with *attentiveness,* or listening with *feedback*). Use this sheet as a reference when giving feedback to the listener.

Listening for Content

- Remembered points the speaker made

- Explained any confusion to the speaker to ensure understanding

- Probed for more information (asked questions such as, "What then?" "What else happened?" "Are there other things I should know?")

- Clarified understanding by paraphrasing back what the speaker said

- Did not interrupt the speaker

Listening for Feelings

- Indicated by body language and/or verbal responses that the listener recognized how the speaker was feeling

- Asked how the speaker felt about what he or she was saying

Listening with Attentiveness

- Maintained good eye contact

- Showed interest with body language (head nods, leaning forward, etc.)

- Asked pertinent and appropriate questions (but didn't over-question)

- Gave responses to indicate interest and/or understanding

- Did not stray from the speaker's subject or take over the conversation

Listening with Feedback

- Showed empathy for what the speaker said or felt

- Checked for understanding when/if confused

- Told the speaker what he or she was thinking or feeling about what the speaker said

- Summarized key points the speaker made

- Responded directly to something the speaker said

25 Activities for Developing Team Leaders. Copyright © 2005 by John Wiley & Sons, Inc. Reproduced by permission of Pfeiffer, an Imprint of Wiley. www.pfeiffer.com

ACTIVITY 14

Using Group Memory
in Team Meetings

Purpose

- To understand the importance of "group memory" in facilitating team meetings

- To list and explain various recording techniques and processes that contribute to effective team meetings

- To practice recording, posting, and using team member inputs during a team meeting

Time

1 1/2 to 2 hours

Group Size

Designed for twelve to twenty-four people

Materials

- Flip chart and marking pens for the facilitator

- Flip chart paper, masking tape, and markers for four teams

- Prepared flip chart with the definition of "group memory"

- One Using Group Memory: Questions for Subgroups posted on a flip chart

- One Using Group Memory: Flip Charts handout per participant

Room Setup

A room large enough for participants to move about freely and confer with one another. Movable chairs should be available as well as plenty of wall space for posting flip charts.

Steps

1. *Introduce the goals of the session.* Ask participants what they think the term "group memory" refers to. After some discussion, show the following definition of "group memory" and compare it to comments made by the participants.

   > *Group Memory:* a collection of thoughts, ideas, decisions, and actions collected from a group of people during a meeting, recorded and posted in such a way that all group members can easily see the material.

   Ask the participants: "What happens when a meeting is held and there is no written record of what was said or decided?" List the responses. Participants will probably come up with some of the following:

   - Ideas are repeated
   - People forget what has already been said
   - Misunderstanding after the meeting
   - Difficult to determine whether actions items have been completed

   Explain that one method facilitators use to lead a meeting is to use flip chart paper to record and post ideas so everyone can see them throughout the meeting.

2. *Explain the subgroup activity.* Tell the participants that they are going to work in subgroups to come up with the *rationale* for using flip chart paper (versus other media) and important *techniques* that will help team leaders facilitate effective team meetings using group memory. Each subgroup will be assigned a different question and will come up with a list of ideas. Each subgroup should appoint someone to be the recorder and write the subgroup's ideas on a flip chart. After two or three ideas have been recorded, the recorder will hand the marking pen to someone else to record. Once each subgroup's ideas are recorded, it will report its findings back to the large group using its flip charts to present the material.

3. *Begin the activity.* Divide the group into *four* subgroups of three to six people each. Have each group find a spot in the room to work and make sure each subgroup has flip chart paper, marking pens, and masking tape. Assign each subgroup one of the questions on the Using Group Memory: Questions for Subgroups sheet. Instruct each group to come up with as many ideas as it can think of and list them on a flip chart and post it in the room.

   After twenty minutes, ask the groups to gather around each subgroup's charts one by one, while the groups report. Begin with question number one and work through all four questions. Ask the appropriate subgroup to report on its list. Ask other groups if they have comments, questions, or additions to make to each subgroup's list. Add any additional ideas. Once all four questions have been addressed, bring the total group back together in a U or semi-circle.

4. *Debrief the activity.* Ask the recorders first what issues they ran into when recording ideas. Ask them what they would do differently next time. Refer the questions back to the large group and ask for suggestions as to how these issues might be handled. Ask the participants what might have helped make the flip charts easier to read or use or to point out what techniques they found particularly effective during their work in subgroups.

   Take a few minutes to discuss recording options other than flip charts, such as white boards, overhead projectors, computer-generated (projected on a screen). Ask the following questions:

   - What other ways can the group memory be recorded besides flip charts?
   - What are some of the main advantages and disadvantages to these methods?

   Note to Trainer: If the following points don't come up in the discussion, point them out when it is appropriate: The biggest disadvantage to white boards is limited space; disadvantages to using an overhead projector are (1) people cannot see several sheets of paper at once and (2) having to turn down the lights makes people sleepy; disadvantages to using a computer are the same as for an overhead projector. Printing notes from a computer or running copies of transparencies gives everyone a look at the material, which can be an advantage in some instances; however, if the group revises or adds to the material, it is best to have one central list that everyone can see. Also, when people are looking at their own notes, heads are down, and there is not the same central focus on the group memory as there is when flip charts are posted. *Whatever recording method is used, it is important that contributors' ideas are recorded quickly and accurately for all to see and that these notes can easily be referred to during a discussion. Also, it is important that the method for capturing ideas allows the group to add to, change, label, or rearrange them.* Encourage participants to record group memory in the most advantageous and useable method available so that the group can work productively. It is difficult to improve on flip charts.

5.   *Distribute the Using Group Memory: Flip Charts handout.* Give participants about three minutes to read over the handout. Ask if there are any ideas on the handout that haven't been addressed already. Mention that during this session the recording was done in *small* groups; ask what recording techniques are important in *larger* groups or for longer, more involved meetings. Ask participants what challenges or difficulties they are likely to run into when attempting to apply these recording techniques in their team meetings. Ask other participants what might be done to overcome these difficulties.

6.   *Wrap up the session.* Review the purpose of the session. Ask for feedback (see "Managing the Group Training Session: Tips for Trainers" in the Introduction, page 11) and adjourn.

USING GROUP MEMORY:
QUESTIONS FOR SUBGROUPS

1. What is the purpose of group memory (or Why use flip charts)?

2. What techniques make flip charts easy to read and refer back to?

3. How can the recorder capture ideas accurately and quickly?

4. How can recorders organize and handle flip charts for easy use during a meeting?

USING GROUP MEMORY: FLIP CHARTS

What is the purpose of group memory? Or Why use flip charts?

- Encourages people to comment
- Portable
- Can be created on the spot
- Focuses everyone on one spot in the room
- Ensures that all ideas are captured
- Objectifies the ideas (keeps them from being associated with a particular person)
- Serves as a reference during future discussions or activities
- Can be used to document the group's actions and decisions
- Several sheets can be posted and viewed at once
- Keeps people from repeating the same ideas over and over
- Increases group productivity
- Can be transcribed as meeting minutes
- Can be reused at future meetings

What techniques make flip charts easy to read and refer back to?

- Print (easier to read than cursive), but *not* in all capital letters
- Use large letters (use whole arm when writing)
- Use dark-colored marking pens for main text
- Use lighter colors for highlighting words or phrases
- Leave space between each line of text
- Use flip chart paper with light blue grids
- Use as few words as possible
- Use bullet points or other indicators (dash, star, arrow, etc.) to indicate where each new idea begins
- Do not crowd the page
- Stand to the side of the easel now and then (so people can read what's written)
- Post flip chart paper on the wall as each sheet is filled

How can the recorder capture ideas accurately and quickly?

- Select key words to capture an idea or thought
- Use speaker's actual words as much as possible (so the meaning is not changed)
- Check with speaker to be sure ideas are captured accurately, if you are not sure

25 Activities for Developing Team Leaders. Copyright © 2005 by John Wiley & Sons, Inc. Reproduced by permission of Pfeiffer, an Imprint of Wiley. www.pfeiffer.com

- Capture all ideas (don't leave anyone's idea out)
- Indicate duplicate ideas in some way (e.g., star ideas that are mentioned by more than one person)
- Use abbreviations to save time (make sure they are common enough for people to interpret them)
- Use symbols in place of words when possible (e.g., a dollar sign for the word "money," an arrow up for the word "increasing" or "rising," etc.)
- Ask for help with spelling
- Ask group to slow down if falling behind
- Include activities that allow participants to help write on the charts
- Ask someone to help post the charts so you can keep writing

How can recorders organize and handle flip charts for easy use during a meeting?

- Title every chart
- Use bullet points to indicate each new idea or thought
- Number the pages
- Change color of marking pen for different discussions, lists, or questions
- Post sheets on the wall in order
- Prepare sheets ahead of time when possible
- If using masking tape, tear pieces ahead of time and stick them to the easel to access quickly when posting the chart
- Use more than one easel
- Use two recorders (especially in fast-paced brainstorming sessions); each recorder writes every other idea
- If using at a subsequent meeting, group sheets together and roll—printed side up—for storage
- Label and date each roll
- Note where they are stored
- If transcribing the charts, do so as soon after the meeting as possible, while ideas are still fresh in the transcriber's mind

Facilitation Practice for Team Leaders*

Purpose

- To understand the value of remaining *neutral* when facilitating
- To identify critical *verbal* and *nonverbal* skills facilitators use to draw out participation and productivity in groups
- To practice verbal and nonverbal skills and receive written and verbal feedback from others in the session

Time

4 to 4 1/2 hours

Group Size

Designed for eight people

Materials

- Pencil or pen for each participant
- One copy of the Basic Facilitation Skills handout per participant

Note: It is important to allow adequate time for this activity, since each participant will lead a ten-minute facilitation followed by time for both written and verbal feedback. Schedule a short meal break about two-thirds of the way through the session. For example, start at 9:00 a.m.; break at 12:00 noon for a 45-minute lunch break; reconvene the session at 12:45 p.m.; and adjourn at 2:15 p.m. Alternatively, hold two shorter sessions on two different days, with the same participants present.

- Seven copies of the Facilitation Practice Observation Sheet for each participant and eight copies for the facilitator

- One copy of Suggested Topics for Facilitation Practice per participant

- Two flip charts with *full* pads of paper and plenty of marking pens in black, dark blue, and other colors

- Masking tape or other method for posting charts

- Name tents for each person

Room Setup

U-shape (see diagram on page 22) with flip chart in the front and an area of free wall space for posting flip charts

Steps

1. *Introduce the session.* Explain the purpose of the session. Make sure participants understand the importance of each person being at all of the session's activities, since all of them will be practicing skills and giving feedback to one another. Explain that the size of the session is kept small to allow plenty of time for practice and feedback, and it is important to have everyone present so there will be an adequate number of people for the discussions.

2. *Lead a discussion on facilitation.* Go to the flip chart and ask the group: "What is a facilitator?" Write the responses on the flip chart, but do not edit them, add to them, or explain them. (You are demonstrating facilitation skills as you lead this discussion.) After a few responses, post this chart and ask the group: "What is a presenter?" List the responses without adding your own comments. Post the second flip chart and ask the group: "What are the key differences between a facilitator and a presenter?" List these responses and use open questions to draw out ideas. Try to get the group to come up with the following ideas: a facilitator's role is to draw out participation and help the group solve problems and make decisions while remaining *neutral* as to what the group decides. A presenter's role is to put forth information, perhaps to persuade others, and to deliver material he or she has organized and summarized. A presenter has opinions and is *not neutral* to the content of the subject at hand. A facilitator may have opinions but does not express these opinions; the role of the facilitator is to guide the discussion and draw out productive participation.

If the group struggles with the concepts, use the material it generated on the flip charts to summarize and point out the concepts. Mention that during the discussion (at least at the beginning), you were acting as a facilitator: asking questions, recording responses, and summarizing ideas.

3. *Introduce basic facilitation skills.* Ask the group to think back on what you were doing during the discussion above. Ask, "What are some things I did to draw out your participation in the above discussion?" List the responses. As the ideas die down, ask the group what other techniques they have seen facilitators use that were effective in drawing out productive participation. List the responses. Post the flip charts in the room as you go, so people can refer to them during the discussion. There may be as many as thirty ideas.

Ask everyone to glance over the ideas they have generated and see if they have listed techniques that revolve around what a facilitator *says,* called *verbal techniques* (such as asking questions, paraphrasing, summarizing, etc.). Use a different color pen to indicate these techniques with a "V." Ask what techniques revolve around what a facilitator *does,* called *nonverbal techniques* (such as use eye contact, position in room, nod head, list ideas on a chart, etc.). Use a different color pen and mark these with "NV." Mention that the nonverbal techniques can be further divided into *body language* and *recording* techniques and point out examples of each.

4. *Discuss facilitation techniques.* Point out that all of these techniques can be used while the facilitator remains neutral on the content of the matter at hand and mention that a good facilitator employs many of the techniques all of the time, so that remaining neutral is a very active job! Be sure everyone understands the difference between an *open* and a *closed question.* Ask participants to come up with some examples of each. Ask the group what effect each type of question has. List on a flip chart the following "magical" words to begin an open question or to elicit an informative response:

- What . . . (What is your response to the survey results?)
- How . . . (How can we be more efficient on this project?)
- Tell me about . . . (Tell me about the conditions that are causing problems.)

Briefly discuss each technique so that there is general understanding. Mention that some of the techniques will be better understood during the practice and feedback sessions later in the activity; don't get bogged down in discussing the techniques at this time. Emphasize the importance of recording people's comments as close to the speaker's wording as possible; in other words, don't paraphrase just to "improve" on what the person said. It's all right to pick out a key phrase or word to record, but not all right to alter the meaning in any way.

5. *Distribute the Basic Facilitation Skills handout.* Go over the list to see if any important skills were not mentioned above. Ask the participants if there are any on the list that need clarifying.

6. *Introduce the practice facilitations.* Explain that the rest of the session will be devoted to practicing some of the techniques discussed above, and that each person will be asked to facilitate a ten-minute discussion on a given topic. Explain that everyone else will participate in the discussion, being their normal selves. At the end of the ten minutes, there will be a brief written and verbal feedback session to point out skills the facilitator used and to suggest other techniques that could have been used. Explain that by not only leading a facilitation but by participating in an active feedback session, each participant's knowledge will be reinforced many times.

   Distribute copies of the Facilitation Practice Observation Sheet and a pen or pencil to each participant (enough for them to complete one Observation Sheet for every other person in the session). Ask each person to silently read over the list of techniques on the sheet so they will know what to watch for. Ask if there are any questions on the meanings of the techniques.

7. *Have participants select skills to focus on.* Ask each participant to determine two or three basic skills they would like to focus on during their own practice facilitation. These should be skills they would like to improve (for example, using open questions, eye contact, remaining neutral, etc.). These can be verbal, nonverbal, or recording skills. Ask everyone to write down the two or three skills they are going to focus on.

8. *Instruct participants to select a topic.* Give each person a copy of the Suggested Topics for Facilitation Practice handout and have each person select a first- and second-choice topic to use when facilitating his or her discussion. Suggest that each participant prepare his or her practice facilitation by thinking of an open-ended question to ask the group to kick off the discussion. Alternatively, ask participants to meet in two small groups for a few minutes and come up with three to five topics suitable for a ten-minute group discussion. List these on a flip

chart and have participants choose from this list. This is effective when team leaders want to deal with real-world issues and gain practical insight from the discussions. If there is a lengthy topic, continue the topic with more than one facilitator, but continue to allow only ten minutes for each person to facilitate.

9. *Lead the practice facilitations.* The order participants facilitate in can be decided in one of the following ways:

   - Let participants volunteer.

   - Draw numbers (participants go in numerical order).

   - Have participants draw colored discs or other items out of a hat without letting you see them. There must be a different color/item for each participant and an identical set of colors/items for you. To determine who goes next each time, draw a color/item. Whoever has that color/item goes next.

   Tell participants that you will call time after ten minutes even if they have not finished. The purpose is not to complete the discussion or come to consensus but to *practice basic skills.* If the discussion comes to a natural conclusion or consensus is reached, that is fine, but not necessary.

10. *Proceed with the practice facilitations.* To make sure every participant leads a ten-minute discussion, use the following process:

    10 minutes: The selected participant facilitates a discussion and records inputs on a flip chart. Do not allow the participant to use a recorder for this exercise. They will be practicing verbal, nonverbal, *and* recording skills.

    3 to 5 minutes: Those who did not facilitate, including you, complete the Observation Sheet. Each participant should keep his or her completed sheet to refer to during the verbal feedback.

    10 minutes: First ask the facilitator to mention what skills he or she chose to focus on and to comment on what went well for him or her during the practice facilitation. (Allow them only to talk about what went *well.*)

    After a minute or so, ask the rest of the participants, "What skills did you see the facilitator use, and what was particularly *effective* about the facilitation?" If someone offers a criticism or suggestion for improvement at this time, interrupt him or her with a reminder to focus on what was particularly *effective* about the facilitation. Use silence to encourage most of the participants to comment. If some do not contribute feedback after one or two rounds, draw them out by asking them what they observed that was effective. It is important for everyone to get experience giving positive feedback, as this is a key facilitation skill. Once participants have commented on what was effective, add your own observations if they are different from ones that have already been made. This is a good time to "teach" the skills by pointing out techniques the facilitator used that were not noticed by the rest of the group.

After several people have commented, ask the practice facilitator to comment on what he or she could have done to be more effective. Do not allow anyone to respond to the practice facilitator's comments at this time. Next, ask the group, "Was there anything this facilitator could have done to make the facilitation even *more effective*?" Again, monitor this activity, but if there are not many comments, don't call on people to add suggestions. Avoid overwhelming the practice facilitator with suggestions for improvement. Two or three are fine. Again, add one or two of your own and use this as a time to "teach" others how to use facilitation skills in certain situations.

Conclude the feedback session by commenting (or asking a participant volunteer to comment) on one thing the facilitator did particularly *well*.

Ask partcipants to pass their completed Observation Sheets over to the person who just finished facilitating.

Each practice facilitation and feedback session will take from twenty to twenty-five minutes. Work in short breaks or a lunch break as needed.

11. *Conclude the session.* Once all practice facilitations have been completed, ask participants to comment on what they learned. If there are still questions or concerns, address them at this time. Review the goals for the session and ask for feedback on the activity (see "Managing the Group Training Session: Tips for Trainers" in the Introduction, page 11) and adjourn.

Note to Trainer

Much of the learning in this activity occurs during the feedback process, both for the person who is receiving feedback and for those giving it. To maximize the benefit of the feedback sessions, it is important to:

- Follow the suggested feedback process for every practice facilitation. Use the same order each time, ask the same questions, and allow about the same amount of time for each person. Encourage people to be specific and caring in their feedback by setting the tone and being an example by your own attitude and comments.

- Ask the practice facilitator to remain in the front of the room (seated is fine) and the rest of the participants to sit in a U-shape, so the practice facilitator can see everyone. You should sit with the rest of the participants.

- Keep the positive and negative feedback separate. Start with the positive.

- Encourage everyone to participate in the feedback process by drawing out quieter members and making eye contact with all the participants when you ask them to give feedback.

- First allow others to give feedback, then add your own comments. It is important that you model giving the type of constructive feedback you want the participants to give. After the first one or two rounds of feedback, participants will become more comfortable and skilled at giving feedback.

- Ask those giving feedback to speak directly to the person receiving the feedback and not "about" them. In other words, coach people not to say, "She used good eye contact throughout her facilitation," but to say (to the practice facilitator), "You used good eye contact throughout your facilitation." You may have to remind participants to do this. Since you are directing the feedback process, participants will be tempted to direct the feedback to you. Just gently remind people to speak to the person receiving the feedback.

- Use the feedback session as an opportunity to teach new techniques and to point out effective uses of techniques mentioned earlier in the unit. Manage the time so everyone has a chance to practice.

Variations

- Lengthen the time of the activity and allow fifteen to twenty minutes for each facilitation. This is a good idea if participants are more experienced team leaders.

- After the first two facilitations, once everyone has learned the process, hand out a slip of paper to everyone except the facilitator for each of the subsequent facilitations. On all of the slips of paper except one or two, write "Be yourself." On one or two slips of paper for each round, write one of the instructions below.

- Disagree with someone else at least three times.
- Be very quiet.
- Give a long or unclear explanation and don't summarize it.
- Talk more than others are talking.
- Ask the facilitator what his or her opinion is.
- Respond two or three times to comments made by others—add to what they have said, or ask them to clarify what they have said.
- Ask someone else in the group what he or she thinks. Do this two or three times.

- If you use this process, there will be one or two people during the practice facilitation playing a role that will add variety and "spice" to the activity and make it more like the real world. If you use this variation, prepare plenty of "Be yourself" slips for all the rounds. Prepare one each of the above instructions and decide as you go along whom you will assign them to. When the practice facilitation and feedback session is complete, ask the role player to reveal what instruction he or she was carrying out.

BASIC FACILITATION SKILLS

Verbal Skills

- Asking questions
- Probing
- Paraphrasing
- Redirecting questions and comments to other people
- Referencing what people have said before
- Giving positive reinforcement
- Drawing in quieter members
- Encouraging divergent views
- Shifting perspective
- Summarizing
- Bridging

Nonverbal Skills

- Active listening
- Tone of voice
- Eye contact
- Showing attentiveness
- Facial expressions
- Silence
- Body language
- Position and movement in the room
- Avoiding distracting habits
- Enthusiasm

Recording Skills

- Use as few words as possible
- Use wording of the speaker (don't alter meaning or add to it)
- Capture all ideas
- When in doubt, ask speaker to summarize
- If not sure, check to see if you captured the idea correctly

- Print large enough for all to see
- Use dark-colored pens for main text; light colors to highlight, number, etc.
- Do not crowd the page
- Use bullet points, dashes, or numbers to distinguish between inputs
- Stand to the side of the easel so people can see the chart
- Post completed charts for reference
- Use abbreviations/symbols to save time (careful not to overdo)

FACILITATION PRACTICE OBSERVATION SHEET

Please answer the following questions by placing a checkmark in the appropriate box.

Name of Observed Person: _____   Your Name: _____

Verbal Techniques	Does Not Do	Does Sometimes	Does Consistently
1. Asking open-ended questions	☐	☐	☐
2. Redirecting questions and responses to other group members	☐	☐	☐
3. Remaining neutral: didn't express opinions on the issues	☐	☐	☐
4. Drawing out quieter group members	☐	☐	☐
5. Seeking differing points of view	☐	☐	☐
6. Using praise and positive reinforcement to encourage participation	☐	☐	☐

Nonverbal Techniques			
7. Limiting distracting movements and nervous habits	☐	☐	☐
8. Focusing attention on the person talking (eye contact, body posture, head nodding, etc.)	☐	☐	☐
9. Using facial expressions wisely (smiles, frowns, etc.)	☐	☐	☐
10. Using silence to pause and give participants time to think	☐	☐	☐
11. Being quiet and allowing participants to respond to one another	☐	☐	☐

Recording Group Inputs			
12. Accurately recording key words and phrases, as close to participant wording as possible	☐	☐	☐
13. Checking with participant, if necessary, to see if his/her inputs have been recorded accurately	☐	☐	☐
14. Writing legibly and large enough for all to see	☐	☐	☐
15. Encouraging participants to summarize lengthy comments	☐	☐	☐
16. Getting help posting flip charts if necessary	☐	☐	☐

SUGGESTED TOPICS FOR FACILITATION PRACTICE

- How are people currently rewarded in your organization? What are the pros and cons?

- What motivates people to work?

- Discuss people's attitude toward work today. How does this compare to what it used to be?

- Discuss both the positive and negative impacts of the Internet on people today.

- In what ways is your organization changing today, and how would you rate these changes: for the better, for the worse, the same?

- It has been said that people are no longer loyal to the company they work for. Do you think that is true? Why?

- Discuss the quality of service you receive as a customer both internally (in your own organization) and externally (outside your organization).

- Who are our heroes today? What makes them "heroes" and why?

- What techniques might you use to deal with a team member who wants no part of teams because teamwork doesn't take the individual into account?

- What career issues are individuals in organizations facing today? Are career opportunities better or worse than they were five to ten years ago?

SECTION 4

AIM FOR CONSENSUS

AN IMPORTANT ROLE of the team leader, in addition to gaining full participation from team members, is to help the team move toward general agreement on important decisions. The team leader's role in building consensus is to bring as many ideas, opinions, and conflicts to the surface as necessary to work toward a satisfactory solution, one that satisfies both the needs of the organization and of the team. Conflict and differences are natural to the work of a team. When a team leader fosters consensus through all aspects of the team's work, team members will learn ways to deal effectively with the inevitable variety of opinions and perspectives present in any given team situation.

Team leaders need to understand what consensus is and is not, when to aim for consensus, and how to structure and direct the consensus process.

Activities in This Section

Activities in this section will give team leaders experience and knowledge in reaching consensus one-on-one, exhibiting and encouraging behaviors that foster an atmosphere of consensus, and using consensus tools in team meetings.

In *Activity 16, Reaching Consensus One-on-One,* participants practice using four steps to reaching consensus in one-on-one situations. Participants work in triads, and each participant plays the role of team leader once, the role of team member once, and the role of observer once. After each role play, participants discuss the role play and give feedback to the participant playing the role of team leader.

In *Activity 17, Guidelines for Reaching Consensus,* participants identify what is *true* and what is *false* about consensus and what behaviors *help* and *hinder* consensus. Participants work in subgroups to gather statements that reflect a particular aspect of consensus. The subgroup that gathers the most correct cards is awarded a prize.

In *Activity 18, Consensus Techniques for Team Leaders,* participants work in subgroups to identify and discuss what team leaders and team members can do to resolve conflict. While one subgroup works, another subgroup observes the interactions and gives feedback on positive and negative behaviors/processes observed.

In *Activity 19, Resolving Conflict: A Consensus Process,* participants receive a team situation, each participant is given a role to play, and the facilitator (instructor) leads the "team" through a process to resolve conflict over the solution. The process for resolving conflict is reviewed and discussed.

Reaching Consensus One-on-One*

Purpose

- To practice reaching consensus with another person (one-on-one)
- To identify skills and strategies team leaders can use to reach consensus in one-on-one situations
- To give feedback to team leaders who are building consensus

Time

2 to 2 1/2 hours

Group Size

Designed for twelve to twenty-four people (three to six subgroups of four people each)

Materials

- Flip chart paper, marking pens, and masking tape
- One Four Steps to Reaching Consensus One-on-One handout for each participant
- One Reaching Consensus Feedback Process Sheet per participant

*Adapted from Help Wanted: Collaborative Problem Solving for Consultants, by Carol Nolde. *The 1992 Annual: Developing Human Resources,* © 1992, San Francisco: Pfeiffer.

- One copy of the Reaching Consensus Role Play Instructions, Rounds 1–4 for each subgroup, cut along the dotted line so team leaders do not know team members' roles and vice versa

- One Reaching Consensus Observer Sheet per participant

- A clipboard or other portable writing surface for each participant

- Paper and a pencil for each participant

Room Setup

A room large enough for participants to work both as a large group and in subgroups of four people each. Movable chairs should be available as well as plenty of wall space for posting flip charts.

Steps

1. *Introduce the goals of the session.* Post two flip charts at the front of the room for all participants to see. On one flip chart write the words "What Consensus Is" and on the other flip chart write the words "What Consensus Is Not." Ask participants to help you complete each chart. Record the responses. Some of the responses will probably be:

   What Consensus Is
   - Agreement to move forward
   - A win-win solution
   - General agreement
   - Hearing everyone's ideas and concerns in relation to the goal
   - Agreement to support a decision 100 percent

   What Consensus Is Not
   - A majority vote/voting
   - A win-lose solution
   - Dictating or forcing agreement

2. *Summarize the participants' inputs.* Make sure all participants understand the definition of consensus: *A point of maximum agreement so action can follow; everyone agrees to support the decision 100 percent.* Emphasize that consensus can be reached even though not all members agree that it is the best way to go.

3. *Distribute the Four Steps to Reaching Consensus One-on-One handout.* Ask participants what skills and strategies team leaders can apply to accomplish each of the steps. Coach the participants to come up with methods, approaches, behaviors, techniques, and skills for each of the four steps. Record the ideas on a flip chart titled "Four Steps to Consensus." To further understanding, ask participants to share examples of when they have seen a team leader use, or neglect to use, one of the steps. What were the results? How might the results have been better if the Four Steps to Reaching Consensus had been followed or more effective techniques or strategies used? Post the Four Steps to Reaching Consensus flip chart along with the participants' ideas.

4. *Introduce the role-play activity.* Explain that, for the rest of the session, participants will be involved in role-playing situations and observing role plays. Explain that the purpose of this is to give each participant a chance to practice one-on-one consensus-building skills and strategies and to give feedback to other participants on their consensus-building skills. Tell the participants that they will each be in a subgroup of four people. In each subgroup and for each role play there will be four roles: team leader, team member, and two observers. The subgroup members will conduct four different role plays, taking turns in the roles so that each participant plays the team leader once, the team member once, and the observer twice. The goal of the role play is to reach consensus. After each role play the observers will share their observations with the role players, concentrating on giving feedback to the team leader. All four members will then discuss the experience, including what the team leader might have done differently to be more effective in reaching consensus one-on-one. Distribute the Reaching Consensus Feedback Process Sheet and ask participants to follow this process after each role play:

    - The team leader makes a few comments about how the role play went for him or her.

    - Observers each give feedback to the team leader on *effective* skills, techniques, and strategies the team leader used.

    - The team member gives feedback to the team leader on what was *effective* about the team leader's skills, techniques, and strategies.

    - Observers give feedback to the team leader on what might have been *more effective.*

    - The team member gives feedback to the team leader on what might have been *more effective.*

5. *Divide the group into subgroups and assign roles.* Assign each participant to a subgroup so that there are four members in each subgroup. Instruct subgroups to decide which two members will participate in the first role play as team member and team leader.

6. *Distribute the Reaching Consensus Role Play Instructions.* Distribute the following to each subgroup: Team Leader Role Play Instructions, Round 1 (to the team leader only); Team Member Role Play Instructions, Round 1 (to the team member only); four Reaching Consensus Observer Sheets; blank paper; pencils; and clipboards (or other portable writing surface). Instruct those playing the roles of team leader and team member to read the roles for Round 1 at this time and to jot down notes about how to play the role. Caution the participants not to discuss the contents of their Role Play Instructions sheet with anyone. Observers should read over the Observer Sheet to prepare for observing the role play, but they should *not* read the role play instructions.

7. *Conduct role plays and feedback.* Ask the subgroups to spend ten minutes conducting the first role play. Observers are to make notes on what they see and hear, using the Observer Sheet as a guide. After ten minutes, stop the role plays and ask the subgroups to spend fifteen minutes on feedback and discussion. Remind subgroups to concentrate on giving feedback to the team leader and to follow the Feedback Process on the handout.

    After the first role play, ask the subgroup members to switch roles and distribute the Reaching Consensus Role Play Instructions sheets for Round 2. Allow a few minutes for each subgroup to prepare for the next role play. Instruct the subgroups to begin the next role play. Continue the role-play exercises until all subgroup members have had an opportunity to be the team leader once, the team member once, and the observer twice, using the Role Play Instructions for Rounds 3 and 4.

8. *Reconvene the total group and debrief the activity.* Allow a short break and then reconvene the large group. Lead a discussion based on the following questions:

    - How productive were the various role plays in terms of reaching consensus?

    - What skills, techniques, or strategies proved to be the most effective in reaching consensus?

- What did the most effective role plays have in common?

- What did the less effective role plays have in common?

- What did you learn about how to be effective as a team leader in reaching consensus with a team member?

- What will you do differently in future consensus-seeking efforts as a result of participating in this activity?

While the participants are discussing the above questions, record those elements (e.g., skills, techniques, strategies, etc.) that were *effective* in reaching consensus and post the ideas in the room for all to see. Have the participants look once again at the Four Steps to Reaching Consensus One-on-One handout. Ask if there are any changes or additions they would like to make to the four steps.

9. *Wrap up the session.* Review the goals for the session. Go around the room and ask participants to state one technique or skill they found particularly useful for reaching consensus. Ask for feedback on the session (see "Managing the Group Training Session: Tips for Trainers" in the Introduction, page 11) and adjourn.

FOUR STEPS TO REACHING CONSENSUS ONE-ON-ONE

1. Draw out the other person's ideas

2. Show understanding

3. Offer one's own ideas

4. Work toward a solution that will meet both people's needs

REACHING CONSENSUS FEEDBACK PROCESS SHEET

1. The team leader makes a few comments about how the role play went for him or her.

2. Observers each give feedback to the team leader on *effective* skills, techniques, and strategies the team leader used.

3. The team member gives feedback to the team leader on what was *effective* about the team leader's skills, techniques, and strategies.

4. Observers give feedback to the team leader on what might have been *more effective*.

5. The team member gives feedback to the team leader on what might have been *more effective*.

REACHING CONSENSUS ROLE PLAY
INSTRUCTIONS ROUND 1

Team Leader

(You will initiate the conversation.) Your role is to come up with an action plan so that the team member you are working with will be more "a part of" the team. He/she tends to stay on the sidelines and is not an "active" member of the team. Several other team members have mentioned to you that he/she does not support the team.

REACHING CONSENSUS
ROLE PLAY INSTRUCTIONS ROUND 1

Team Member

Your role is to get the team leader to understand why you don't become involved more with the team: you have a heavy workload, with much of your work being done on your own. Much of the time you find the team meetings and the effort to work closely with others gets in the way of your own work.

REACHING CONSENSUS
ROLE PLAY INSTRUCTIONS ROUND 2

Team Leader

(You will initiate the conversation.) You want to encourage the team member to speak up more at team meetings. You know he/she has a lot of information and experience in relation to the current team projects; however, he/she is quiet and hesitant to speak up in meetings. You want to find out why and provide some support, if possible.

REACHING CONSENSUS
ROLE PLAY INSTRUCTIONS ROUND 2

Team Member

You are usually somewhat quiet at team meetings. Although you have excellent knowledge and experience in relation to the current team projects, you feel somewhat intimidated by others on the team who are very outspoken, articulate, and used to working together. You are fairly new to the team and have yet to feel really comfortable with that group of people.

REACHING CONSENSUS
ROLE PLAY INSTRUCTIONS ROUND 3

Team Leader

Your role is to try to reach consensus with the team member as to how he/she can feel more a part of the team and work closer with other team members. He/she is one of two team members who work in a different location from the others on the team. You are concerned because lately he/she has not been attending all of the team meetings and, according to other team members, has not worked as closely with them as they would like. Now he/she is approaching you with some concerns.

REACHING CONSENSUS
ROLE PLAY INSTRUCTIONS ROUND 3

Team Member

(You will initiate the conversation.) You are concerned that team members who work together at a different site from you are not taking you seriously. When you try to connect and collaborate with team members to get your work done, it seems that it is always inconvenient for them to meet you at the site where you work, ten miles away. You are tired of always having to go to the other site because you have an extremely full workload and don't want to waste time. You are beginning to feel like an outsider to the team, but you really need to work closely with other team members if you are going to make your deadlines.

REACHING CONSENSUS
ROLE PLAY INSTRUCTIONS ROUND 4

Team Leader

(You will initiate the conversation.) You have recently lost a team member who was transferred to another location. You need to have someone else take on some extra work for the time being, at least until you can replace that team member. You have asked to see one of your most loyal and efficient team members to see if he/she will take on the extra work.

REACHING CONSENSUS
ROLE PLAY INSTRUCTIONS ROUND 4

Team Member

You are a loyal and efficient team member and have always taken on all the tasks you can handle for your team. However, lately you have been feeling that your personal life is not what you would like it to be. You simply work too much of the time. Over the weekend you attended a self-development work-shop, which inspired you to begin building more of a balanced life for yourself. You are looking forward to some changes you plan to make.

REACHING CONSENSUS OBSERVER SHEET

Answer the questions below as you observe the role play. You will use this same sheet for both rounds that you are an observer.

How well did each person draw out and listen to the ideas/thoughts of the other?

Specific examples:

How well did the *team leader* show understanding of the *team member's* point of view?

Specific examples:

How well did the *team member* show understanding of the *team leader's* point of view?

Specific examples:

Did each person offer his/her own ideas and suggestions regarding the issue?

Specific examples:

How well did the team leader and team member work toward a solution that would meet both people's needs?

Specific examples:

Guidelines
for Reaching Consensus

Purpose

- To identify what is *true* and what is *false* about consensus
- To identify practices and behaviors that *hinder* and *help* consensus

Time

1 to 1 1/2 hours

Group Size

Designed for twelve to twenty-four people (four subgroups of three to six people each)

Materials

- Flip chart paper, marking pens, and masking tape
- A bell
- Forty-eight 4 x 6 cards, each with one statement from the Statements About Reaching Consensus sheet printed on it, *without* the answer. Cards should be shuffled to ensure random distribution to four subgroups (twelve cards per subgroup). *Note to the trainer:* When preparing the 4 x 6 cards, show the number of the statement. This will make it easier to find the answers during the game.

- Four prizes, one for each subgroup: first, second, third, and "booby" prize (optional)
- One copy of the Statements About Reaching Consensus handout per participant

Room Setup

A room large enough for participants to work both as a large group and in subgroups of four people each. Movable chairs should be available as well as plenty of wall space for posting flip charts.

Steps

1. *Introduce the goals of the session.* Divide the participants into four subgroups of three to six people each. Explain that each subgroup is going to gather statements that reflect an aspect of consensus. *Do not discuss consensus before beginning the activity.* First, instruct each subgroup to meet and decide on its definition of consensus. Ask the subgroups to write their definitions of consensus somewhere so that only members of their subgroup can see it. Explain that they will use this definition in the gathering of statements in the next activity. Allow about five minutes.

2. *Give instructions for the activity.* Read the following instructions to all the subgroups:

   "Each subgroup will be given a set of twelve 4 by 6 cards, each with a statement on it about consensus. Some of the statements are *true*; some are *false*; some refer to a practice or behavior that *helps* reach consensus; some refer to a practice or behavior that *hinders* consensus. Your subgroup will be assigned one of these four types of statements—true, false, helps, or hinders. Your goal is to trade cards with other subgroups until you have gathered all of the statements in your assigned category. For example, if your subgroup is assigned the 'false' category, you will trade your cards with other subgroups until you collect only those statements about reaching consensus that are false. Cards must be traded one for one. Subgroups do not have to stay together; individuals can move around and contact members of other subgroups as desired. However, it is a good idea to reconvene now and then with your subgroup to check progress and strategies. When your subgroup has collected all the cards in its category, one of the subgroup members should come forward and ring the bell. When the bell rings, all subgroups must stop their trading. The subgroup that rang the bell then reads off its statements. If all statements are correct for that subgroup's category, that subgroup wins a prize. When a subgroup has one or more incorrect statements for that category, the trading begins again and no prize is awarded for that round. Rounds will continue until all subgroups have collected the correct set of cards for their categories, or until time is called."

Explain that you, the facilitator, will determine whether a subgroup's statements are correct or not as the game proceeds. Discussion of the statements will occur later. Allow plenty of time for participants to trade; however, when the trading dies down, call time and have each subgroup read its cards aloud. The important thing in this activity is to build awareness about consensus: what it is, what it is not, and what practices and behaviors foster consensus.

3. *Conduct the activity.* Make sure everyone understands the directions. Explain that each subgroup should use its own definition of consensus when determining what statements to gather to support its categories. Assign each subgroup a category: false, true, helps, or hinders. Begin the trading. Walk around the room and clear up any confusion that may result. If a subgroup rings the bell, stop the trading and ask all subgroups to return to their areas. Ask the subgroup that rang the bell to read its cards one by one. Do not allow other subgroups to comment on whether the cards are right or wrong at this time. If a card is wrong, announce only that it is wrong; don't state what category it belongs in. If the subgroup has gathered all the correct cards, award a prize. If the subgroup wins a prize, it must wait out the next rounds as each subgroup finishes collecting its cards. If the subgroup does not gather all the correct cards, it must return to the trading again.

Finish the rounds and award the prizes.

4. *Discuss the results.* Distribute the Statements About Reaching Consensus handout and lead a discussion with the following questions:

   • Were there any designations that you do not agree with? Why?

   • Would you change any of the categories?

   • What can team leaders do to help their teams foster an atmosphere of consensus?

   • How might team leaders use these statements in their teams?

5. *Wrap up the session.* Review the goals for the session. Ask participants to look at statements in the Helps category (from the Statements About Reaching Consensus handout) and select one statement that represents a practice or behavior they rate as highly important for teams in reaching consensus. Go around the room as each participant reads the statement he or she has selected. Thank the participants for their participation. Get feedback on the session, if desired (see "Managing the Group Training Session: Tips for Trainers" in the Introduction, page 11) and adjourn.

STATEMENTS ABOUT REACHING CONSENSUS

The following are statements about reaching consensus. Some of the statements are *false*; some of the statements are *true*; some represent techniques or behaviors that *help* reach consensus; and some represent techniques or behaviors that *hinder* reaching consensus.

1. To reach consensus, everyone must agree 100 percent that the decision is the best one. (False)

2. Discuss the merits of each idea. (Helps reach consensus)

3. When people disagree on which decision is best, it's OK to vote; simple majority wins. (Hinders reaching consensus)

4. When people listen carefully to one another, this builds an atmosphere for consensus. (True)

5. Arguing for your own solutions. (Hinders reaching consensus)

6. Consensus results in a win-win situation. (True)

7. When people compromise, they are helping the consensus process. (False)

8. Consensus is reached when everyone can support the decision 100 percent. (True)

9. A team is more likely to reach consensus if it is clear what goal everyone is striving for. (True)

10. When consensus is reached, no one had to give in on any strongly held convictions or needs. (True)

11. Being open-minded, not antagonistic, toward new ideas. (Helps reach consensus)

12. Being secretive and closed about one's motivations, feelings, fears, and hopes. (Hinders reaching consensus)

13. Consensus seekers find ways for all parties to get what they want. (True)

14. Be friendly and caring even if it is at the expense of seeking the truth or the best solutions to problems. (Hinders reaching consensus)

15. Show equal respect for all team members and ideas. (Helps reach consensus)

16. Discourage provocative and imaginative thoughts and comments. (Hinders reaching consensus)

17. Digress—get off the subject. (Hinders reaching consensus)

18. Harbor a hidden agenda or ulterior motive—don't let others know what you are really trying to achieve. (Hinders reaching consensus)

19. Confronting an idea is offensive, and doing so means you are being critical of the person who contributed the idea. (False)

20. Don't put forth your opinion unless asked. (Hinders reaching consensus)

21. Recording people's ideas is too time-consuming and should be avoided if possible. (False)

22. Stick to the subject at hand. (Helps reach consensus)

23. Don't interrupt others when they are talking. (Helps reach consensus)

24. If everyone comes to agreement early on, this is a good sign. (False)

25. For the sake of reaching consensus, it is a good idea to hold back your ideas and opinions if they are quite different from those already put forth. (False)

26. Recording group decisions on a flip chart for all to see. (Helps reach consensus)

27. Building consensus takes more time initially, but in the long run, consensus means more support and commitment from those who must make something happen. (True)

28. Consensus is always the best strategy. (False)

29. "Group think" is the tendency for team members to place high priority on agreeing with one another. (True)

30. "Group think" encourages creativity and frequently leads to a superior decision. (False)

31. If you know the issue ahead of time, it is a good idea to work out a solution of your own before the meeting. (False)

32. Compromise or change your mind in order to avoid conflict. (Hinders reaching consensus)

33. Support only those decisions you can live with. (Helps reach consensus)

34. Consensus does not always result in a better quality decision or outcome. (True)

35. Groups can unanimously agree on a completely incorrect solution to a problem. (True)

36. Using rational decision processes such as brainstorming, fishbone diagramming, decision matrix, etc. (Helps reach consensus)

37. Using a planned process, clear instructions, and a skilled facilitator. (Helps reach consensus)

38. Aim for a majority decision as soon as it is evident that there is not unanimous agreement. (Hinders reaching consensus)

39. Individuals are better at solving problems than groups. (False)

40. It is not a good idea to give examples to support your point. (False)

41. Honest commitment of the leader to the group's decision. (Helps reach consensus)

42. Agreement on the procedures and methods for decision making prior to deliberation on the issue. (Helps reach consensus)

43. A classroom style room arrangement for a meeting to reach consensus. (Hinders reaching consensus)

44. Keep everyone in one large group all the time. (Hinders reaching consensus)

45. When team members are committed to reach consensus, they are more apt to be open-minded and creative. (True)

46. If everyone agrees too quickly, ask if anyone has a different opinion. (Helps reach consensus)

47. It is important to remain objective during the process and not be sensitive to others' feelings and needs. (False)

48. It is a good idea to set ground rules (norms) before starting to reach consensus. (True)

Consensus Techniques for Team Leaders

Purpose

- To identify tips and methods team leaders can use to set up an atmosphere for consensus and resolve conflict in teams
- To experience a team consensus process using a "fishbowl" process

Time

1 1/2 to 2 hours.

Group Size

Designed for ten to fourteen people

Materials

- Flip chart paper, marking pens, and masking tape
- One Consensus Techniques for Team Members handout for each participant
- One Consensus Techniques for Team Leaders and Facilitators handout for each participant
- One Consensus Techniques Observer Sheet for each participant
- Pencils for participants

Room Setup

U-shape (see diagram on page 22). A room large enough for participants to work both as a large group and in two subgroups of five to seven people each. Movable chairs should be available as well as plenty of wall space for posting flip charts.

Steps

1. *Introduce the session.* Distribute the Consensus Techniques for Team Members handout. This list specifies what team *members* can do to help their teams resolve conflict. Explain that, during this session, participants will come up with a list of things *team leaders* can do to help teams resolve conflict. Ask each person to read over the list. Point out that team leaders can also do these things to help the team resolve conflict, but that there are additional things team leaders can do to help develop an atmosphere of consensus and resolve conflict.

2. *Conduct a "fishbowl" exercise.* Divide the group into subgroups of five to seven people each. Bring one subgroup into the center of the U-shape and ask the other subgroup to remain outside the tables to observe. Hand out the Consensus Techniques Observer Sheets and pencils to the outer group. Instruct the subgroup in the center (the "fishbowl") to spend ten minutes brainstorming ways *team leaders can help their teams resolve conflict.* They can include processes, behaviors, methods, etc. Remind them that brainstorming means idea generation only, not discussion. Suggest that someone record the ideas on a flip chart. Instruct observers to answer the questions on the Observer Sheet.

   After about ten or fifteen minutes, interrupt the subgroup in the fishbowl and instruct them to decide *five* of the most effective ways team leaders can help their teams resolve conflict. Tell the subgroup to try to reach consensus. Allow about twenty minutes for this part of the activity. Ask the subgroup to post its five top ideas on a flip chart.

3. *Debrief the activity.* Lead a discussion of what happened during the activity. First, ask those in the fishbowl the following questions:

   - What did members of your subgroup do to help your team reach consensus?
   - How well did your team do in reaching consensus?
   - What could it have done differently?
   - How do you feel about the quality of the top five ways you selected?

Next, ask the observers to comment on the following:

- During the first part of the activity, did the subgroup stick to the brainstorming process?

- Give examples of what subgroup members did to help the group reach consensus.

- Were there any conflicts to resolve? If so, how were they resolved?

- Did the group have a team leader? What might have been different if the group had selected a leader? If the group did have a leader, what did the leader do to help the team achieve consensus?

- If you were the team leader of this team, what would you do to help the team reach consensus?

4. *Conduct another fishbowl exercise.* Switch the two subgroups so that the observers are in the fishbowl and the first team becomes observers. Hand out Observer Sheets and pencils to the new observers. This time, the subgroup in the fishbowl must come up with five new ideas to add to the first list. Allow ten minutes for brainstorming; interrupt the subgroup and ask it to reach consensus in the same fashion as the first group did.

5. *Debrief the activity.* Lead a discussion similar to the first one. This time, ask what advantages the second fishbowl group had, since it had the opportunity to observe the first group.

6. *Add to the lists.* Look at the two lists generated by the fishbowl subgroups that show the most effective ways team leaders can help their teams resolve conflict. If the groups reached consensus, there will be about ten ideas. Ask the large group to evaluate the ideas and to discuss the relative merits of the ideas. Ask the group which of the ideas they feel comfortable or skilled at using and which of the ideas they need help/training to use effectively.

7. *Wrap up the session.* Distribute the Consensus Techniques for Team Leaders and Facilitators handout. Let the participants look it over. Tell them that this sheet represents only a few suggestions but they may be helpful additions to the lists they generated today. Ask volunteers to collect ideas generated by the two fishbowl teams and distribute them to the participants after the session.

8. *Review the goals for the session.* Ask for feedback on the session, if desired (see "Managing the Group Training Session: Tips for Trainers" in the Introduction, page 11) and adjourn.

CONSENSUS TECHNIQUES FOR TEAM MEMBERS

- Keep the end goal in mind. Help others do the same.

- If people seem unclear about the goal, ask members to review the goal.

- Listen carefully to *understand* the other person's ideas (not to judge them).

- Find merit in the other person's viewpoint.

- Review the speaker's main points in your mind as he or she speaks.

- State the other person's viewpoint back to him or her to show you understand.

- Restate another's idea if you did not understand it the first time.

- Avoid defending your own view until you have fully understood the other person's view.

- Don't hold back when you disagree or have another idea.

- State your own view clearly, firmly, and without being overly emotional.

- When interrupted, ask people to let you finish making your points.

- Once you have been heard, avoid harping on your own position. Let your idea stand on its own merit.

- Try not to get attached to your own position. Keep the end goal in mind and don't take it personally if the team decides to go with another approach.

- Offer suggestions instead of simply rejecting someone else's approach.

- View team conflict as natural and help your team work toward a mutually agreeable solution that will satisfy as many of everyone's needs as possible.

- Show sensitivity to others' needs and feelings.

- Show equal respect for all members and ideas.

- Once consensus is reached, follow through with actions that support the decision.

CONSENSUS TECHNIQUES
FOR TEAM LEADERS AND FACILITATORS

- Provide guidance and clear direction regarding team goals.

- Set up structures and processes that will help the team resolve issues.

- Make sure team members keep the goal in mind.

- Help the team develop its own guidelines (norms) for resolving conflict.

- Use proven team processes, tools, and techniques for brainstorming, problem solving, decision making, and analysis. Using these methods helps teams address conflict naturally as part of the work of the team.

- Focus people on the ideas, not on personalities behind the ideas.

- Help the team determine whether a disagreement is central to and important to the team's progress, or peripheral and not so important to the team's progress.

- Allow time for all ideas to be heard, understood, and considered.

- Encourage brainstorming and innovative suggestions.

- Help team members understand that conflict is healthy and can lead to innovation and problem solving.

- Encourage team members to bring things into the open for the whole team to solve, not to harbor things and discuss them in "cliques."

CONSENSUS TECHNIQUES OBSERVER SHEET

Instructions: Put a check mark beside any item you see in operation during the fishbowl exercise. Watch for both positive and negative behaviors/processes. Make notes to help you remember specific incidents (for later group discussion).

Positive Behaviors/Processes Observed

- Finding merit in another's viewpoint
- Stating another person's view back to him or her
- Stating a view clearly, firmly, and without being overly emotional
- Keeping the goal in mind
- Offering suggestions instead of criticizing
- Working toward a mutually agreeable solution
- Looking at many ideas and several perspectives
- Being open about one's own needs and feelings
- Showing equal respect for all members and ideas
- Showing tolerance and using humor and other tension-relieving activities
- Encouraging and respecting imaginative, creative, and unusual thoughts and comments
- Disagreeing without being offensive (focus on the idea, not the person)

Negative Behaviors/Processes Observed

- Getting off the subject
- Dominating the conversation
- Acting disinterested
- Being overly disagreeable, without offering solutions
- Being overly positive (not seeing potential problems or pitfalls)
- Interrupting others before they can make their points
- Not listening well to others
- Being prejudiced, narrow-minded, or set on one's own solution
- Harping on one's own position; mentioning it over and over
- Pushing people to agreement before ideas have been heard
- Ignoring the overall goal
- Refusing to offer suggestions that promote a win-win for everyone
- Disagreeing with others' suggestions as to a solution

Resolving Conflict:
A Consensus Process

Purpose

- To experience a consensus process
- To identify specific methods for resolving conflict and reaching consensus in groups

Time

2 to 2 1/2 hours

Group Size

Designed for twelve to sixteen people

Materials

- Flip chart paper, marking pens, and masking tape for each subgroup
- One copy of the Resolving Conflict Situation Sheet per participant
- Enough Resolving Conflict Role Descriptions sheets for one role per participant, cut so that no one sees another person's role description; if there are fewer than sixteen participants, distribute the roles so that there is a fairly equal distribution of opinions
- One Resolving Conflict Process handout per participant

Room Setup

A room large enough for participants to work both as a large group and in two subgroups of six to eight people each. Movable chairs should be available as well as plenty of wall space for posting flip charts.

Steps

1. *Introduce the goals of the session.* Tell participants they are going to participate in a consensus seeking activity. Explain that you will be the facilitator and will try to use various methods and approaches to help the group resolve conflict over an imaginary situation they will be given as a team. Tell participants that at certain times during the activity, you will stop the process and ask them to reflect on certain aspects of group process in relation to resolving conflict. Explain that the group will be given a situation to solve as a team and that each person will receive a role definition. Each person should try to play his or her role as true to the role as possible while using his or her normal personality traits. (There is no need to be an "actor.") Explain that the goal of the activity is to reach consensus—to come up with a decision or position of agreement that everyone can support 100 percent.

2. *Distribute the Resolving Conflict Situation and the Resolving Conflict Role Descriptions (one role per person).* First distribute the situation and read it aloud to the group. Next distribute the roles, one per person. Ask each person to read his or her role carefully and imagine he or she is part of the team that will be resolving where to locate the team members' offices.

    Open the discussion by announcing that you have been asked to facilitate the meeting and that the goal of the meeting (or possibly two meetings) is to come up with a solution as to where their offices will be located. The decision needs to be made this week, since the team begins its new project next month and arrangements will need to be made so that everyone has an office. Tell participants that they should play their roles with the intent of eventually coming to a workable consensus with the team. Tell them that each person has a chance to influence the outcome.

3. *Begin the role play.* Lead a discussion, opening with the question: "What suggestions do you have about where our offices should be

located? I'd like to know how everyone stands on the issue and why." Let the group talk and don't record their comments. Keep asking questions to try to draw everyone out, including the quieter members. The goal is to get people to share where they stand.

4. *Form two groups.* After most/all people have commented, stop the discussion and acknowledge that there are obviously different opinions on the issue at hand. Ask participants to form two groups at this time: those who prefer working from a company office and those who prefer working from home. Those who are neutral or undecided can join either group. Give each group a flip chart and marking pens. Have them meet in separate sections of the room. Instruct the subgroups to list all the reasons they can think of that *the other group gave for its position.* In other words, the subgroup favoring working at the office must list the reasons they heard for working at home, and vice versa.

5. *Read lists groups have created.* When the writing dies down, bring the groups together and have each group read its list to the other. After one list is read, ask the other group if that group captured its reasons well. Why or why not? Once each group has read its list and the other group has commented, ask if either group wants to have the other group list any more reasons. If so, make sure each group has listed *all* the reasons of the *other* group. (This part of resolving conflict is to make sure both sides have truly heard one another.)

6. *Mix up the subgroups and review the goals.* Instruct the two subgroups to "mix up" and form two new subgroups with a mix of opinions in each group. Each subgroup should select about half of its members to join the other group. Give the following instructions:

   • Write what you think are the *goals of the other group.* What are they hoping to achieve? What motivates them?

   • Write what *your own group's goals* are. What are you hoping to achieve? What motivates you and your group?

   Explain to the new subgroups that they now have the task of coming up with an *overall* goal, a *common* goal that both groups share. Allow about five to ten minutes for each subgroup to write a common goal and post it in the room. Bring the groups back together and see if the goals are similar. If not, see if the large group can come up with one or two goals that everyone can agree on. (Be sure the goals are not stated in the form of a solution, but in the form of an overall goal everyone is aiming for.) Write the goal(s) on a flip chart.

Next, ask if anyone has changed his or her opinion, or if any of the more neutral people are moving in one direction or another. If so, ask them to tell why they have changed their minds.

7. *Debrief the process.* Stop the process for a while and debrief what has occurred so far. Ask participants the following questions to stimulate discussion and reflection:

   - How did you feel during the first discussion? Did you feel heard? Were your ideas ignored or considered?

   - How did you feel when the other group was listing your reasons? Did you feel they were respecting your thoughts or simply writing them down out of obligation?

   - How did you feel when you were working with a subgroup to determine the overall goal? Was this a productive session? Why or why not?

   - So far, how productive do you think your team has been using this process?

   - What do you think the team should do next?

   Note: If you are facilitating a large group of participants (or they are all fairly talkative), divide them into groups of three or four people each for this discussion. Then bring the small groups back together and have them summarize the answers to their questions.

8. *Brainstorm solutions.* Point out that the next step in this process, once a common goal is established, is to brainstorm solutions. Ask everyone to write down as many solutions as he or she can think of. Go around the room and have each person state his or her ideas. (Since you are demonstrating the process, don't take time to write out the ideas. However, point out that during real brainstorming the ideas should be written and posted.) Point out how many creative ideas have flowed just from this process. Ask the group what it would do next to move toward consensus.

9. *Distribute the Resolving Conflict Process handout.* Point out that the process the group just went through is the first half of this process. If there is time, or if the group wishes, work through the rest of the process during the training session. If not, simply discuss how a team leader would lead a group through the process.

10. *Wrap up the session.* Review the goals for the session. Ask participants to each share one insight they had during today's session. Ask for feedback on the session (see "Managing the Group Training Session: Tips for Trainers" in the Introduction, page 11) and adjourn.

RESOLVING CONFLICT SITUATION SHEET

You are a member of a team that has been asked to start up a new division of the company you work for. Your management has picked each of you because you have worked successfully together in the past. You are trusted, loyal employees who all have worked hard for your company. Some of you are currently with other divisions and at different facilities. Your offices are currently scattered among three facilities.

Your new division is supposed to become a profit center of its own in two years, and your goal is to make it profitable in that amount of time. The first two years will require a lot of research, planning, and dedication to get the new division off the ground. Both team and individual work will be required, some of it creative and some of it more tedious.

Your company does not have room for all of your offices at its current location. Management has suggested that some or all of the new team can be set up to work out of their homes, at least for a period of time until new offices can be located. Another manager even suggested that working from home will save money and help the division move toward profitability. Your direct-line manager, however, would prefer that you all work on-site together, even if you have to double up on offices. Your manager is convinced that you will be a better team if you are located in the same area. However, doubling up on office space would mean that you have less space than you really need to work. You do know that once the division is up and running, you will all need offices from which to work because you will undoubtedly have others reporting to you by then.

Since management is busy and in a quandary as to where to house all of you at this time, your manager has asked that you hold one or two meetings and come up with a solution that will support the organization's long-term goal of profitability in two years.

RESOLVING CONFLICT ROLE DESCRIPTIONS

Role #1. You are against having any of the team members work from home. You have worked with "teams" before who were at different locations, and you believe it hurt the team. It was simply too difficult to get everyone together as frequently as necessary, and the work stalled as a result. There was not enough co-worker interaction and support.

Role #2. You were ecstatic when you heard some of your team members might get to work from home. You have always wanted to be out of the sterile work/office environment. You believe you would be more creative at home and would serve the team better there. You would have some peace and quiet in which to do your creative work.

Role #3. You definitely do not want to work from home. You have worked out of your home before and got fed up with all the hassles: namely, having your work life infringe on your home life (phones and faxes ringing, working at night, work problems bringing stress into the home, equipment problems to deal with, etc.). You would miss the daily camaraderie and support of your co-workers. You will definitely push for not having to work at home!

Role #4. You are somewhat neutral about the issue. You think it might be kind of novel to work at home, something new and different. In fact, it would be nice not to have that rush-hour commute in the mornings and evenings. However, you think you would miss the hustle and bustle of the office environment and would certainly miss hanging out at lunch and coffee breaks with some of your teammates. You will look at both sides of the issue, try to remain objective, and do what is best for the company.

Role #5. You would really love to work from home for a while. One of your children is young and you could be home when he gets home from school. You envision that you could build your workday around the needs of the family, leaving the easier administrative work until the afternoon and some of the tedious work for evenings when your son is doing homework. You could set up your office in one corner of the rarely used living room.

Role #6. You know that working from home would be difficult for you. Teenagers coming and going there night and day make it difficult to concentrate. You are also short on space and don't know where you would set up an office. However, you are not particularly happy about squeezing into a cramped office space with some of your co-workers. You don't have much reason to work so closely with any of them, and some of them would make it almost impossible for you to get anything done! You think the company should spring now for offices and adequate space for all of you, since that is what you are going to need in two years anyway.

Role #7.   Your main concern is working up in the organization. You want to have a highly visible role on this team and in the future with the company. You definitely want to work at the offices where the other managers are, but you don't mind if some of the team works at home. For you, teamwork is simply a way of getting ahead in the organization.

Role #8.   Be your "real self" in this role play and act as you would if presented with this situation.

Role #9.   You are fairly neutral on the situation. You are going to listen objectively to everyone's argument and help everyone look at all sides of the situation. You believe that once all sides of the issue have been considered, the group will see the best way to go. You like to point out things others have overlooked.

Role #10.   You definitely would like to work at home and don't think it will hurt the productivity of you or the team. You know that most of the team members will be glad to meet at opportune places whenever needed. Your life would be improved greatly if you could work from home. You would not have that long 30- to 40-minute commute each way daily. You could go into the office as needed during the middle of the day. You already have a home office set up that you could use. Your spouse travels a lot, and no one is home during the day. The dog is very lonely, and no one is there when someone needs to come do a repair or delivery. Yes, working at home is the answer for you!!

Role #11.   You simply could not work at home! Your spouse works at home and there is no more room left for another work-at-home person. In fact, you know that working at home together would probably have you at each other's throats in no time. Both of you are hard-driving, ambitious business people with separate lives of your own. This is important in your marriage. Working together is simply out of the question!

Role #12.   You are convinced that for the team to be productive and pull off this goal of profitability in two years, most of the team members need to work out of the same location. If people worked at home, they would have to do much of the administrative work, and this would slow down progress on their own work. At the office, there is an excellent and loyal administrator whom the team can rely on. You might consider having one or two of the team members work at home for one or two days a week, but for the most part, you think the team needs to be together.

Role #13.   You are not going to get too involved in this issue. No one on the team or in the company knows this yet, but you are planning to take another job in two months. You will be joining a small start-up company in California with an old friend of yours, and you will be working from home while your two children are still young. You are fed up with going into an office every day and worrying about your children. Your spouse has already found a position in California and will begin commuting there within two weeks. You are going to be selling your home and tying up things here. You can't bring this up in the meeting, however, since you haven't talked with your manager about it. You are waiting until the last minute because you don't want to quit before your spouse is into the new job.

Role #14.   You think this whole thing is silly. Why even discuss the complications of setting everyone up in their home offices when in less than two years they will have to be moved back into offices? As for some working at home and others not, you think this could become a nightmare of communication problems, liability issues, lack of productivity, etc. You also don't trust two or three of the team members to be at home working. They will probably be out golfing or at the mall, returning their messages later in the day. You wish the meeting were over because you think it is a waste of time.

Role #15.   You are new to the team and don't want to rock the boat. You will go along with whatever the team decides. However, you have worked out of your home before and have some firsthand experience with both the pros and cons of doing so. You are also aware of the pros and cons of working in an office. No place is perfect. You will do your best to help the team reach a win-win for the company and the team members both.

Role #16.   You are excited about the upcoming project and think it could prove to be a chance for advancement in your career. Furthermore, you like most of the team members and don't want to get on the "bad side" of any of them. Plus, you don't really have a backup plan if this project fails. Since you are the key "breadwinner" in your family, you need to provide well for your spouse and three children. Your main goal is to find a solution that means the team will do a great job on this project! You are a motivated worker and can work almost anywhere if you have the necessary tools. You are a natural team player and will see to it that you stay connected to your team-mates, even if you are not working in the same location.

RESOLVING CONFLICT PROCESS

This process can be used when people are divided into two or more "camps" on an issue. The purpose is to make sure each side hears and understands the points presented by the other side. It involves writing out (or repeating back) what the opposing side has said. The turning point is when all sides have heard one another out and together they come up with a common goal, one that everyone agrees they will work toward. From then on, the process follows traditional brainstorming, discussion, and prioritization processes until the group comes to a joint, win-win solution.

- Step *One*: Announce the situation/problem to the group. Lay out as many facts and as much data as is necessary to prepare the group to make a decision.

- *Step Two*: Lead a discussion to find out where people stand on the issue. What do they think is the solution? Try to draw everyone out. Ask people not to get into discussions at this time but simply to state their opinions and ideas. Do not record the ideas, since you will be asking the groups to do that in Step Three.

- *Step Three:* Break into groups based on viewpoint and have groups feed back (in writing or verbally) to one another what they have heard the "opposing" sides say. It is a good idea to have the ideas written out on a flip chart for everyone to see. Ask these groups not to berate the ideas or reasons of the other side, but to show they have heard and understood the other side's point of view. They are not agreeing with it; they are demonstrating their skill and maturity in *hearing and understanding.*

- *Step Four:* The groups then give feedback to the presenters, letting them know whether they presented their opinions accurately and whether any were left out. If any were left out, the presenting group should write these down in the words of the person(s) whose idea/opinion it is. During this step, it is important that all sides have their ideas written out/heard accurately. Discussion is still not allowed, other than to clarify that the ideas have been heard accurately.

- *Step Five:* Form subgroups that are mixed, with members from various sides in each subgroup. At this point people will be working together whose opinions differ. Each subgroup comes up with what it thinks is the overall, common goal of all sides of the issue. Subgroups must take into account the organization they are serving, as well, if this is the case. Each subgroup presents its goal statement to the other groups, and the facilitator works with all subgroups to determine the common goal of the group.

- *Step Six:* Once a goal has been agreed on, the entire group brainstorms as many solutions as it can think of to reach the goal, taking into account the arguments posed by all sides. Follow a traditional brainstorming process so that all ideas are presented first without discussion, discrediting, or reinforcement.

- *Step Seven:* Clarify the brainstormed ideas, eliminate any that are unworkable, and discuss the merits of the remaining ideas.

- *Step Eight:* Use a prioritization process to find the top few ideas that are the most appealing to the group.

- *Step Nine:* Evaluate the top ideas, perhaps testing them, and collect further data if desired.

- *Step Ten:* Decide as a group on which idea is the best, combining more than one idea or rejecting all ideas and looking for a better one.

SECTION 5

DIRECT THE PROCESS

A KEY RESPONSIBILITY of team leaders is to guide the process of helping team members to work together productively. The process of teamwork centers around two dimensions: social and task. An effective team leader is focused on providing ways for both dimensions to be addressed.

The *social* dimension focuses on *how team members work together as a team.*

Helping the team work together as a unit, increasing the ability of team members to work productively together, and giving the team opportunities to grow stronger as a team—all of these support the *social* success of a team. The social dimension acknowledges that team members need to effectively interact with one another while showing mutual respect and tolerance of one another's different experiences, expertise, and style. This dimension acknowledges that good teamwork requires ways of communicating and collaborating that build trust and openness within the group.

The *task* dimension focuses on *what the team members accomplish as a team.* Helping the team organize and manage its tasks, seeing that work is done in a timely and effective way, and achieving a balance of support from all team members—all of these support the *task* dimension of teamwork. An effective team leader needs a kind of blueprint or map that guides the team through its various activities step by step. Leaving out steps, or diminishing the importance of any step, can hurt the team's progress.

Activities in This Section

The activities in this section focus on helping team leaders develop a well-functioning team through understanding of the stages of team development, giving and receiving feedback, solving team challenges, and working with the team to evaluate itself. The last exercise gives team leaders a tool to identify and develop strategies for areas they would like to develop, improve on, or change in relation to their role as a team leader.

Activity 20, Understanding the Stages of Team Development, reviews the four stages of team development—forming, storming, norming, and performing—and identifies the team characteristics associated with each of these stages. Participants work in teams to identify the stages of various team characteristics, points are awarded, and the winning team receives a prize.

Activity 21, Team Leader's Role in the Stages of Team Development, reviews *five* stages of team development and discusses the team leader's role in each of these stages. (While Activity 20 focused on the four classic stages of team development, some literature refers to a fifth stage, which Tuckman called "Adjourning," called "Transforming" in this activity.) Participants work in pairs to review a case study and answer questions in relation to stages of development and team leader challenges presented in the study.

Activity 22, Feedback Awareness: Skill Building for Team Leaders, develops participants' awareness of the impact of feedback on team leader performance. Participants receive guidelines for giving and receiving feedback and work with partners to practice feedback skills.

In *Activity 23, Solving Team Leader Challenges,* participants collaborate with one another to select the best tips and strategies for dealing with various team leader challenges. Participants work in quads (teams of four people) through several rounds of discussion. Over the course of the activity, the quads are divided up so participants work with a variety of different people.

In *Activity 24, Evaluating Team Health,* participants are given a sample Team Health Questionnaire and work in teams to select the fifteen items from the questionnaire that would be the most useful to a team when evaluating itself. Next, participants receive guidelines for conducting a team self-evaluation, and the teams follow these guidelines to evaluate their teamwork.

Activity 25, Managing Growth of a Team Leader, helps participants zero in on their own areas of strength as team leaders and identify areas that need improvement. Each participant completes a Team Leader Self-Evaluation Form and discusses the results with another participant. Next, each participant selects one or two priority areas to address and develops goals, an action plan, and long-term strategies for improvement in those areas.

Understanding the Stages of Team Development*

Purpose

- To review four stages of team development
- To identify various team characteristics associated with each of four stages of team development

Time

2 hours

Group Size

Designed for twelve to twenty-four people

Materials

- Flip chart paper, marking pens, and masking tape
- One Stages of Team Development handout per participant
- One Stages of Team Development Item List per participant
- One Stages of Team Development Record Sheet per participant
- One Stages of Team Development Correct Classification List for the facilitator

*Adapted from "Stages, Reviewing the Team-Development Process" in *Teamwork and Teamplay: Games and Activities for Building and Training Teams* by S. Thiagarajan and G. Parker, 1999, San Francisco: Pfeiffer.

- Pens or pencils for participants
- Prizes (optional)

Room Setup

A room large enough for participants to move about freely and confer with one another. Movable chairs should be available as well as plenty of wall space for posting flip charts.

Steps

1. *Introduce the goals of the session and review the stages of team development.* Distribute one copy of the Stages of Team Development to each participant. Go over the the four stages with the group.

2. *Distribute the items to be classified.* Give a copy of the Stages of Team Development Item List and a pen or pencil to each participant. Explain that these items are related to behaviors, attitudes, thoughts, feelings, perceptions, expectations, problems, strategies, and tactics associated with the four stages of team development. Ask the participants to review the first two items and identify the stage associated with each. Review the first two items with the group and show how the first item belongs to the performing stage and the second belongs to the norming stage.

3. *Form teams and explain the rules of the game.* Divide the group into small teams of three to four people each. Distribute a copy of the Stages of Team Development Record Sheet to each team. Explain the rules of the game as follows: "You will call out an item number. All teams will review that item number with their team members, identify the stage of team development it is associated with, and record the appropriate abbreviation on the record sheet. If the item is associated with more than one stage, record all of them."

4. *Explain the scoring system.* After the teams have been given a maximum of one minute to record an answer, you will announce the *official* answer (based on the opinions of a panel of experts and shown on the Stages of Team Development Correct Classification List) for the item. Each team that selected the correct stage will receive 1 point. Each team will also receive an additional point for each of the other teams that missed the official answer. Each team will record its points in the "game points" column of the Team Development Record Sheet.

5. *Begin the first round.* Randomly call out an item number. (Mark the number you have called out so you will not repeat it.) Ask the teams to discuss the item, select the appropriate stage (or stages) in the team-development process, and write down their choice on the Team Development Record Sheet. Circulate among the teams and clarify the procedure if necessary. Check to see that teams have recorded their responses. If a team holds up the progress of the game, give it a ten-second time limit to finish.

6. *Announce the official response.* When all the teams have recorded their responses, refer to your Correct Classification List and announce the officially determined stage.

7. *Award points.* Instruct the teams to award 1 point for selecting the correct answer and 1 additional point for each team that selected the wrong answer. For each round, announce to the entire group how many teams selected the wrong answer and instruct the teams that selected the correct answer to add these points to their records. *Those teams that selected the wrong answer will have 0 points for that round.*

8. *Continue the game.* Repeat the above procedure of calling out an item number, asking the teams to record the appropriate stage, announcing the experts' answer, and computing the scores.

9. *Announce a pause for planning future rounds.* At the end of the fifth round, tell the teams to spend the next three minutes planning for future rounds. They can use this time to consolidate what they have learned, to review the item list, and to determine playing strategies. After three minutes, resume the game as before and finish calling out all of the remaining items.

10. *Conclude the game.* Once all the items have been called out and scored, ask the teams to add up their scores. Identify and congratulate the winning team. (Present the winning team with a prize, if desired. Remember to have extra prizes on hand in case of a tie.)

11. *Debrief the activity.* Ask the participants to discuss what they learned from playing this game. Here are some suggested questions to stimulate the discussion:

    • Which stage is the most difficult one to understand and to apply?

    • Why can it be difficult to assess which stage a team is in? What are some important clues to look for?

    • What can happen to cause a team to repeat a stage(s)?

- Can a team be in two stages at the same time? Why or why not?

- Can any of the stages be divided into two (or more) narrower stages? How? Why?

- Are there additional stages that should be added to the process of team development? What stages? Why?

- How does this information help a team leader increase his or her effectiveness?

- How would you apply this information to the team you are currently leading?

Variations

- Impose a time limit for each round. For example, ask the teams to come up with the correct classification within sixty seconds.

- If the teams differ in their classifications, ask each team to justify its response. Permit teams to change their original classification, if desired. However, points will still be awarded based on the official experts' answers.

STAGES OF TEAM DEVELOPMENT

Psychologists who study the behavior of small groups suggest that all teams go through four distinct stages in their development. Although these stages have been given different terms, B.W. Tuckman's (1965) four terms are probably the most common: *Forming, Storming, Norming,* and *Performing.*

1. The first stage in a team's development is *Forming*. During this stage, the team members are unsure about what they are doing. Their focus is on understanding the team's goal and their role on the team. They may be unsure or uncomfortable around one another. They worry about whether the other team members will accept them. Team members frequently look to their leader for clarification during this phase.

2. The second stage in a team's development is *Storming*. During this stage, the team members try to get their act together and to solidify goals and roles. This stage is marked by conflict among the members and between the members and the leader. Through this conflict, the team attempts to define itself.

3. The third state in a team's development is *Norming*. Once the team members have resolved some of their basic issues during the storming phase, they now feel more secure with one another and with their leader. They effectively work through the structure of the team, agree on standards of operation, and determine the various duties for which team members will be held responsible.

4. The fourth stage in a team's development is *Performing*. During this stage, the team members behave in a mature fashion and focus on accomplishing their goals. This stage is marked by direct, two-way communication among the team members; collaboration and cooperation to achieve the team's goals; and by the team's increasing ability to monitor itself and solve its problems.

Reference

Tuckman, B.W. (1965). Developmental sequence in small groups. *Psychological Bulletin, 63*(6), 384–399.

STAGES OF TEAM DEVELOPMENT ITEM LIST

1. All members participate in all team activities.

2. Disagreements become more civilized and less divisive.

3. Feeling of "us vs. them" increases.

4. Ground rules become second nature to team members.

5. If there is a formal leader, team members tend to obey him or her.

6. Leadership is shared among different members.

7. Leadership role is rotated among appropriate members.

8. Members are anxious and suspicious of the task ahead.

9. Members are more committed to their subgroups than to the team as a whole.

10. Members are more friendly toward one another.

11. Members are concerned about how their individual needs will be met on the team.

12. Members are not fully committed to the team goal.

13. Members are proud to be chosen for the team.

14. Members are relieved that things are progressing smoothly.

15. Members are satisfied about the team progress.

16. Members argue with one another, even when they agree on the basic issues.

17. Members attempt to figure out their roles and functions.

18. Members begin to enjoy team activities.

19. Members challenge, undermine and/or ignore other people's ideas.

20. Members choose sides.

STAGES OF TEAM DEVELOPMENT RECORD SHEET

Round	Item Number	Stage	Game Points
1			
2			
3			
4			
5			
6			
7			
8			
9			
10			
11			
12			
13			
14			
15			
16			
17			
18			
19			
20			

STAGES OF TEAM DEVELOPMENT
CORRECT CLASSIFICATION LIST

Item Number	Stage
1	P
2	N
3	N
4	P
5	F
6	N, P
7	N, P
8	F
9	S
10	N, P
11	F
12	F
13	F
14	N
15	P
16	S
17	N
18	P
19	S
20	S

Team Leader's Role in the Stages of Team Development

Purpose

- To review five stages of team development
- To discuss the team leader's role in each of the five stages
- To analyze case studies of teams in relation to the five stages of team development

Time

2 to 2 1/2 hours

Group Size

Designed for fifteen to twenty-five people.

Materials

- Flip chart paper, marking pens, and masking tape
- One Team Leader Role Worksheet per participant
- One Team Leader Stages of Team Development Matrix per participant
- One Team Leader Case Study per participant
- Pens or pencils for participants

Room Setup

A room large enough for participants to move about freely and confer with one another. Movable chairs should be available as well as plenty of wall space for posting flip charts.

Steps

1. *Introduce the goals of the session and review the stages of team development.* Post a flip chart showing the five stages of team development as follows:

   (1) Forming

   (2) Storming

   (3) Norming

   (4) Performing

   (5) Transforming

   Do not hand out the Team Leader Stages of Team Development Matrix at this time. Guide the participants through a brief discussion of the five stages.

   Point out that some material works only with the more classic first four stages of group development. (The previous activity in this book, Activity 20, focused on those four stages.) Some group specialists, however, include a fifth stage to reflect the moving on or adjourning phase of a team's life. In this activity, participants will work with all five stages.

   Ask participants to give examples of the characteristics of each stage. Help them if they are not sure. Explain that the "Transforming" stage is brought on by goals or activities that mark the ending or the re-forming of the team. During the transforming stage, the team can look back on its efforts, appreciate its accomplishments, and acknowledge either the disbanding or the renewal of the team. If the team is renewing, it is a good time to formulate new goals, review membership, and figuratively start a "new" team. If the work of the team is finished, it is a good time to mark the ending of the team with some kind of ritual or ceremony, a time to acknowledge the team's efforts and accomplishments, and give team members a chance to say goodbye to fellow teammates.

2. *Give instructions for the team activity.* Announce that you will divide the group into five teams of equal size. The task of each team will be to review *one* of the five stages in relation to the role, behaviors, and tasks required of the team leader to navigate this stage of the team's development. Distribute a copy of the Team Leader Role Worksheet and a pen or pencil to each person. Divide the group into five teams and assign each team one of the stages to work on. Briefly go over the questions they will be answering from the Team Leader Role Worksheet. Post a flip chart in the room for all teams to see during the activity. On the flip chart, write the words Role, Behaviors, Tasks, Challenges, and Actions to focus the groups on the assignment.

3. *Conduct the activity.* Allow thirty to forty-five minutes for this activity. Instruct the subgroups to answer the questions on the Team Leader Role Worksheet and prepare to discuss their answers with the rest of the group. Check in with the teams from time to time to clarify any confusion or answer questions. Instruct teams to prepare a flip chart listing their answers to the questions. Ask them to select a spokesperson to present the answers back to the large group.

4. *Give team presentations.* Bring the teams back together and have each team present its answers. Go in order from Forming through Transforming. After each team presents, ask the rest of the group if there are any questions, comments, or additions to the information presented by that team. Discuss these as necessary. Emphasize that there are no hard-and-fast answers for these questions and that each team may require a somewhat different approach. Team leaders can use their knowledge of the stages of team development as a guideline, but should always adapt their approach to the unique needs of their team.

5. Distribute the Team Leader Stages of Team Development Matrix. Explain to the participants that this handout was developed to instruct and to help team leaders think about the various aspects of team development. Ask participants to look over the section of the handout titled "Leader's Role" to see if they overlooked anything during their previous discussions. Ask if there are any items they would like to discuss, that they disagree with, or that they might like to add. Next, direct the participants' attention to the section titled "Team Members' Role." Ask if there are any items they would like to discuss, that they disagree with, or that they might like to add.

Next, ask them to look at the section titled "Pitfalls" and explain that often a team gets stuck in a particular stage and that it is the team leader's role to intervene and guide the team to move forward. Lead a discussion on the following questions:

- Have you been on a team that got stuck in a particular stage?

- What stage was the group stuck in, and what happened?

- What might the team leader have done to move the team forward?

After a few examples have been shared, ask the participants what stage they think is the most difficult to move a team out of. Why? Ask what the team leader can do to guide the team forward. List the responses on a flip chart.

6. *Review the case study.* Distribute the Team Leader Case Study and ask individuals to read the case silently to themselves. Ask participants to work in pairs and ask each pair to respond to the two sets of questions included in the case study. Allow pairs about fifteen minutes to formulate and write down their responses.

7. *Debrief the case study.* Bring the group back together and go over the pairs' responses to the two sets of questions. Once all responses have been read, ask the participants the following questions:

- What suggestions struck you as being particularly useful?

- What suggestions would you find difficult to implement? Why?

- What did the suggestions have in common?

- Were there any suggestions that were particularly unique or innovative? In what way?

8. *Wrap up the session.* Review the goals for the session. Go around the room and ask each participant to name one idea or suggestion he or she will be able to take back to work with his or her own team as a result of today's activity. Ask for feedback on the session (see "Managing the Group Training Session: Tips for Trainers" in the Introduction, page 11) and adjourn.

TEAM LEADER ROLE WORKSHEET

1. How would you describe the *role* of the team leader during this stage of the team's development? Justify why you chose this role. Choose from the following, or come up with a role description of your own: *Visionary, Director, Facilitator, Teacher, Coach, Sponsor, Consultant.* (Note that the team leader may have to fulfill more than one role during a given stage of development.)

2. What *behaviors* are the most important for the team leader to exhibit during this stage of the team's development?

3. What *tasks* must the team leader fulfill during this stage?

4. What *challenges* might the team leader face during this stage?

5. What one or two *actions* can the team leader take to work through these challenges?

TEAM LEADER STAGES OF TEAM DEVELOPMENT MATRIX

	1. Forming	2. Storming	3. Norming	4. Performing	5. Transforming
Characteristics	Politeness Tentative joining Membership may be unstable Orienting personally and professionally Gathering impressions Avoiding controversy Hidden agendas Cliques may form Need for safety and approval	Struggles over purpose and goals Vying for leadership Differences in points of view and personal style become evident Lack of role clarity Reliance on voting, arbitration, leader-made decisions Team organizing itself and its work	Cohesion, harmony Balanced influence Open-minded Trust builds Comfortable with relationships Cliques dissolved Focus and energy on tasks Planning *how* to work as a team Confidence and creativity high	Team fully functional Roles clear Interdependent Team able to organize itself Flexible Members function well individually, in subgroups, or as a team Empathy for one another	Internal or external forces bring about *renewal, change,* or *dissolution* Momentum slows down Activities mark the ending or renewal of team efforts
Team Identity	Individual identity prevails	Individual identity still strong; team identity begins to build	Team identity emerges	Team identity strong	Team identity dissolves or renews
Leader's Role	*Visionary/Director* Provide structure and clear task direction Allow get-acquainted time Create atmosphere of confidence, optimism Active involvement	*Facilitator/Teacher* Acknowledge conflict Guide toward consensus Get members to assume more task responsibility Teach conflict-resolution methods Offer support and praise Active involvement	*Coach/Sponsor* Give feedback and support Plan celebrations Allow for less structure Continue to focus on building strong relationships Less involvement	*Consultant/Sponsor* Give positive reinforcement and support Offer consultation Keep channels of communication open Share new information Allow team to organize itself and to test new procedures	*Facilitator/Visionary* Help team develop options for renewing or disbanding Guide the process Help team design its "rituals" for renewal or ending Offer sincere appreciation for team's accomplishments

	1. Forming	2. Storming	3. Norming	4. Performing	5. Transforming
Team Members' Role	Ask questions to get clear about team's initial tasks Avoid cliques Get to know each member Have patience with the process Listen Suspend judgment	Consider all views Initiate ideas Aim for synergy Help team reach consensus on goals, purpose, roles Build solutions from everyone's needs Accept conflict as natural Respect diversity of team members	Take responsibility to influence *how* team works Keep a realistic outlook Avoid harmony for sake of harmony Be flexible Support efforts to build "team spirit" Initiate and consider new ideas	Keep goals in mind Maintain flexibility Continue consensus process Complete action items Provide information to team Support and verify team norms Keep momentum going	Accept need for team to "move on" Participate fully in efforts to *end* or *renew* team Help evaluate team's success Carry forth learning to next team effort
Pitfalls (Ways to Get Stuck in This Stage)	Staying too polite Lack of clear direction	Lack of conflict-resolution skills No one to facilitate conflict resolution Individuals stuck on own agendas "Turf wars" and "tree hugging"	"Groupthink" Comfort Focus too much on relationships, ignore tasks Unwilling to take risk External change that may alter team's purpose	"Burnout" Team not evaluating and/or correcting itself Lack of training OK to stay here if productive	Failing to renew when it's time Renewing too soon Unwilling to disband team when its work is done Not honoring the *process* of transforming
Bridge to Next Stage	Adequate comfort level	Collective "win"	Confidence, risk taking	Reflection, evaluation	A definite ending, change, or renewal
Conflict	Low	High	Low	Healthy conflict (team has learned ways to resolve differences)	Low
Output	Low	Low	Low to Medium	High	Temporarily tapers off or ends

Source: Based on Bruce Tuckman's classifications of the stages of group development (1965). Tuckman's fifth stage is called "Adjourning." © 1997 Rees & Associates. From "Developmental Sequence in Small Groups," by B.W. Tuckman. *Psychological Bulletin,* Vol. 63, pp. 384–399. Used by permission.

TEAM LEADER CASE STUDY

The As You Like It Print Shop is a small department that supplies its company (a large, nationwide moving company) with all of its printed materials, including advertising and promotional materials, company annual reports, monthly newsletters, presentation booklets, and training manuals. All of its customers are internal to the company. The AYLIPS (As You Like It Print Shop) has a reputation for doing good quality work, even though it doesn't always give customers a timely turnaround. Customers within the company who use AYLIPS often wish they could go outside to get work done, especially when they need something done quickly.

Recently, AYLIPS was assigned a new manager, a highly experienced and creative manager, Joe Wordsworthy, who came from a top-notch publishing firm. Joe was hired to update the print shop and to work with its employees to become a high-performing team, namely, to make it more responsive to the dynamic needs of the company. The firm Joe comes from has been noteworthy in its successful use of self-managed teams.

After a few weeks on the job, Joe discovered that no one was cross-trained and that each person specialized in one area of the work. If someone was out sick or on vacation, progress slowed down. When talking to employees about this, he got the impression that each person did quality work but did not want anyone else to infringe on his or her "territory." Many of the employees had been with the company for many years. Some barely spoke to one another as work was passed along from person to person with instructions written on worksheets.

After three or four meetings, Joe explained that he would like the people to think more like a team. He worked with them to form a mission statement and publish that statement to the organization. He noticed that some people were quite enthusiastic about some of the new ideas; others were holding back. Some didn't even show up to the meetings. Many kept working just as they had before.

Discussion Questions

1. What stage of development is the team in? How do you know?

2. What challenges does Joe face to move the team on to the next stage?

3. What should he do to see that this particular stage is complete before moving on to the next stage?

A few months later, the AYLIPS had become more of a team. Team members were working more closely together. There had been quite a lot of disagreement at some meetings over changes in how work was shared and passed from person to person. However, many of these disagreements were settled. A couple of the team members admitted to Joe that they were dissatisfied because they had been in line for Joe's position. Joe suggested they volunteer to head up some of the team's subgroups, especially those that were working to make changes in the way work was done. This would give them experience in leading teams.

Some members were still not very cooperative, but the team as a whole had identified several goals to accomplish over the next six months. Team meetings were inconsistent. Sometimes they went well, sometimes they did not. A few more cooperative team members worked to hold the team together. Others seemed to come along for the ride. One of the team's biggest projects was due in a few weeks, and Joe wanted all of the team members to work together on it. He thought this would be a great way to solidify the team. Yet he was apprehensive. It seemed that the team members didn't all have the same sense of ownership to the team as a whole.

Discussion Questions

1. What stage of development is the team in? How do you know?

2. What challenges does Joe face to move the team on to the next stage?

3. What should he do to see that this particular stage is complete before moving on to the next stage?

Feedback Awareness: Skill Building for Team Leaders*

Purpose

- To develop team leader awareness of the impact of feedback
- To practice giving and receiving feedback

Time

2 hours

Group Size

Eight to sixteen people

Materials

- Flip chart paper, marking pens, and masking tape
- Pencil and clipboard, or other portable writing surface, for each participant
- One Feedback Awareness Worksheet per participant
- Two copies of the Feedback Awareness Communication Sheet for each participant
- One Guidelines for Giving and Receiving Feedback per participant

*Adapted from Feedback Awareness: Skill Building for Supervisors, by Robert William Lucas. *The 1992 Annual: Developing Human Resources,* © 1992, San Francisco, CA: Pfeiffer.

Room Setup

A room large enough for subgroups to work without disturbing one another. Movable chairs should be available as well as plenty of wall space for posting flip charts.

Steps

1. *Introduce the goals of the session.* Explain that giving and receiving feedback is an important team leader skill. Effective feedback given to the team and to team members can steer the team in the right direction and avoid serious pitfalls later. Team leaders also need to be open to receiving feedback, since this will help them understand their team and become better all-around team leaders.

   Tell participants that this activity will help them:

   - Identify their strengths and weaknesses in *giving* feedback

   - Identify their strengths and weaknesses in *receiving* feedback

   - Identify *improvements* they would like to make in giving and receiving feedback

   - *Practice* giving and receiving feedback

2. *Discuss individual likes and dislikes regarding feedback (Section I).* Distribute the Feedback Awareness Worksheet, clipboards, and pencils and ask participants to work individually for a few minutes and complete Section I. Meanwhile, label two flip charts, one with the title "I Don't Like" and the other with the title "I Prefer." After participants have had time to write several responses, go around the room and have each participant contribute one response at a time until you have about ten responses for each of the two categories. To summarize, ask participants to make some general statements about how people *prefer* to receive feedback, based on the above responses. Ask participants: "What can you conclude about things to *avoid* when giving feedback, based on these responses?"

3. *Discuss team leader responses regarding giving feedback (Section II).* Next, ask participants to think about how they give feedback to others. Ask them to take time individually to respond to the statements in Section II of the Feedback Awareness Worksheet. After several minutes, divide the group into pairs and have pairs discuss their responses to Section II with one another.

4. *Partners give feedback to each other.* Distribute two copies of the Feedback Awareness Communication Sheet and one copy of the Guidelines for Giving and Receiving Feedback to each person. Explain that each person will give feedback to the other person on his or her communication techniques during the previous discussion of Section II of the worksheet. Instruct the pairs to do the following:

   - Read the Guidelines for Giving and Receiving Feedback individually.

   - Individually complete one of the Feedback Awareness Communication Sheets to assess how your partner communicated with you during the above exercise. Be sure to name at least *three* things the other person did well in his or her communication and *one* thing that could be improved.

   - Using the Feedback Awareness Communication Sheet you have just completed, give feedback to your partner, based on the communication techniques he or she used during the above exercise.

   - Switch so that each person gives feedback to his or her partner.

5. *Switch partners.* Once each person has both given and received feedback, have pairs switch to find other partners and do the next activity.

6. *Discuss team leaders receiving feedback from team members (Section III).* During this round of the activity, instruct pairs to discuss the questions in Section III of the Feedback Awareness Worksheet.

7. *Pairs prepare short presentations.* Ask each pair to prepare a short presentation of their conclusions using a flip chart. Allow about twenty minutes for this preparation. Bring the group back together and have the pairs give their presentations. Summarize what was said during the presentations.

8. *Partners give feedback to each other.* Reconvene the pairs who gave the presentations. Ask each pair to give feedback to one another on their communication techniques during the discussion of Section III of the Feedback Awareness Worksheet (Step 6). Use the same method as before (first write the comments on the Feedback Awareness Communication Sheet, then give feedback verbally).

   Say that each person should name at least *three* things the other person did well in his or her communication and *one* thing that could be improved. Allow about ten minutes. Bring the group back together.

9. *Debrief the feedback activity.* Bring the total group together and lead a discussion on the following questions:

- How did you feel when you heard comments about your own communication techniques after each of the two discussions?

- How did you feel when you made comments about the other person's communication techniques after each of the two discussions?

- On the basis of your experience during this activity, what, if any, barriers interfered with the feedback process?

10. *Wrap up the session.* Review the goals for the session. Go around the room and ask each person to respond to the following questions (post the questions in the front of the room):

- What have you learned about your own abilities to give and to receive feedback?

- How might you improve your abilities to give and receive feedback?

Ask for feedback on the session (See Managing the Group Training Session, page 11). Adjourn.

FEEDBACK AWARENESS WORKSHEET

Section I

List as many responses as you can think of to each of the following statements:

1. When *receiving* feedback from someone, I *do not like* feedback that is. . . .

2. When *receiving* feedback from someone, I *prefer* feedback that is. . . .

Section II

List as many responses as you can think of to each of the following statements:

1. When *giving* feedback to someone, I try to use the following *skills or tactics*:

2. When *giving* feedback to someone, I wish I could *be better* at. . . .

3. I am most *comfortable* giving feedback when. . . .

4. I am *least comfortable* giving feedback when. . . .

Section III

What suggestions do you and your partner have for team leaders if they want to receive quality feedback on their team leadership from their team members? What *actions, behaviors,* and *strategies* can they use to ensure they will receive quality and timely feedback from their team members?

What actions, behaviors, and strategies should team leaders *avoid* if they want to receive quality feedback from their team members?

FEEDBACK AWARENESS COMMUNICATION SHEET

Instructions: Write your name and your partner's name in the blanks provided. Answer the questions, jotting down any specifics that might be useful to your partner. Then describe at least *three* of your partner's communication *strengths* and identify *one* area for *development*.

Your Name: _____ Your Partner's Name: _____

During the conversation, did your partner:

1. Use clear language?

2. Speak at a rate you could easily follow and understand?

3. Use specific rather than general terms?

4. Check with you to see if you understood?

5. Pay attention when you spoke?

6. Maintain good eye contact?

Name at least *three* of your partner's communication strengths:

1.

2.

3.

Name *one* communication area for development:

GUIDELINES FOR GIVING AND RECEIVING FEEDBACK

Guidelines for Giving Feedback

- Be objective in describing the behavior.

- State specific details, not generalities.

- Deal only with behavior than can be changed.

- Describe the impact of the behavior on you.

Guidelines for Receiving Feedback

- Keep an open mind; be willing to hear ways to improve.

- Listen without interrupting, justifying, or explaining.

- Paraphrase the feedback so that the person who gave it can determine whether you understood the intended message.

- If you do not understand, ask for an example or further explanation.

Solving Team Leader Challenges*

Purpose

- To create a list of challenges team leaders face
- To discuss tips for dealing with these challenges
- To collaborate with other participants to select the best tips for dealing with team leader challenges

Time

2 to 2 1/2 hours

Group Size

Designed for eight to twenty-four people

Materials

- Flip chart paper, marking pens, and masking tape
- 3 x 5 index cards, seven per participant
- A pencil for each participant
- A bell

*Adapted from SDLT, A Self-Directed Learning Team Activity, in *Teamwork and Teamplay,* by S. Thiagarajan and G. Parker. © 1999. San Francisco: Pfeiffer.

Room Setup

A room large enough for participants to move about freely and confer with one another. Movable chairs should be available as well as plenty of wall space for posting flip charts.

Steps

1. *Introduce the goals of the session and begin the activity.* Distribute seven 3 x 5 cards and a pencil to each participant. Ask participants to work individually and write down *up to seven* challenges team leaders face when leading teams. If participants think of more than seven, tell them to choose the seven most typical or most important challenges. Participants should write *one* challenge per card. Allow about five minutes for this activity.

2. *Pairs review the challenges.* Divide the group into pairs and have the partners in each pair review the challenges they selected and weed out any duplicates. Discard the duplicate cards. They are not to discuss the challenges at this time except to weed out redundancies.

3. *Quads review the challenges.* Next, have two pairs join together to form a quad (four people). Each pair should bring its set of 3 x 5 cards along. Instruct each quad to go over the challenges shown on its cards and, again, weed out any redundant challenges.

4. *Select challenges.* Finally, have each quad select *four* challenges to work on in today's session. Explain that the rest of the session will be spent working out tips and strategies for dealing with these team leader challenges. Bring the entire group back together and, one at a time, ask each quad to read aloud the four challenges it selected. As each quad reads its list, it should eliminate any challenges that have already been mentioned by other quads. Once all challenges have been read, ask each quad to once again read its challenges and ask people to "vote" for a total of *three* challenges they would like to discuss and develop tips and strategies for. Ask for a show of hands as each challenge is read. Ask the quad members to keep track of how many people raised their hands for each of the challenges it read. Select the top seven challenges (depending on the time available) to work on for the rest of the session and list these top seven challenges in order, placing the challenge with the highest number of votes at the top and so on.

5. *Develop tips and strategies: Round One.* Starting with the challenges that had the most votes, take each challenge one at a time and do the following:

    a. Work in *pairs* to list the four or five most likely causes or contributing factors to this challenge. For example, if the challenge is "unproductive team meetings," the contributing factors or causes might include lack of facilitators, people leaving early or arriving late, etc.

    b. Join another pair and work in a *quad* to compare notes from the activity just completed. (If there is an odd number of pairs, three of the pairs may join one another to form a group of six.) Discuss tips and strategies that might help team leaders meet this challenge.

    c. When you hear the bell, take three minutes to select two or three of the best tips and strategies to report back to the entire group.

6. *Present the results.* Bring the entire group back together and have each quad report its best tips and strategies. This is the end of Round One. During Round One, all the pairs and quads worked on the same challenge.

7. *Develop tips and strategies: Round Two.* This time, have people pair up with someone they have not yet worked with. Repeat the process used in Round One, this time selecting another one of the top challenges voted on by the group. When pairs join into quads, have them try to find people they have not worked with before.

8. *Conduct Round Three.* This time, give the participants the choice of either continuing to work as they have been, one challenge at a time, or doubling up and working on two challenges at a time. (There must be at least eight participants to do this.) If the participants choose the doubling up method, divide the group into pairs and assign one half of the pairs one challenge and assign a different challenge to the other half. (Once again, select the higher-ranked challenges from the voting process above.) This time, when a pair joins another pair, it must join a pair that is working on the same challenge.

9. *Conduct Round Four and so on.* Let the participants decide whether to continue working on one or two challenges at a time. Continue until the time is up or at least five and up to seven challenges have been worked on.

10. *Debrief the activity.* Ask participants to take a few minutes to recall the different tips and to jot down personal notes about two or three of them for immediate application back on the job. Lead a discussion of the activity using the following questions as a guide:

- What are some common themes that emerged among the tips and strategies?
- What was the most useful tip for each topic?
- Did you contribute your fair share of tips? If not, why not?
- What are the advantages and disadvantages of developing tips and strategies in this manner?
- How might this process be used with a team?

11. *Wrap up the session.* Review the goals for the session. Ask for feedback on the activity (see "Managing the Group Training Session: Tips for Trainers" in the Introduction, page 11) and adjourn.

Variations

- Speed up the activity by reducing the number of topics, reducing the time allotted to each round, or by asking the participants to work in pairs only, skipping the formation of quads.
- Repeat the session at another time and work on more of the topics, starting with the topics that got the next-highest number of votes, and so on.
- Tell participants that team leaders can arrange to work on their own without a trainer using this process.
- A different person can be assigned during each round to record the tips and strategies and distribute them to participants after the session. Make sure the challenge for each set of tips and strategies is clearly labeled.
- Team leaders can use this process with their teams to help the team come up with solutions, tips, and strategies for its own issues.

Evaluating Team Health

Purpose

- To discuss what makes a "healthy" or effective team
- To understand the value of having team members evaluate their team
- To receive and discuss a Team Health Questionnaire that can be adapted for use by a team
- To practice conducting and participating in a team self-evaluation

Time

2 1/2 hours

Group Size

Designed for twelve to twenty-four people (three to six subgroups of four people each)

Materials

- Flip chart paper, marking pens, and masking tape
- Flip chart prepared ahead of time of the Advantages of Periodic Team Self-Evaluations (or use as a handout or overhead transparency, if desired)
- One Team Health Questionnaire per participant
- One Guidelines for a Team Self-Evaluation per participant
- Pens or pencils for participants

Room Setup

U-shape (see diagram on page 22)

Steps

1. *Introduce the goals and topic of the session.* Ask participants what they think are the key components of a "healthy" or effective team. List responses on a flip chart for all to see.

2. *Discuss team self-evaluation.* Explain that today's session will be focused on team self-evaluation. Post the prepared flip chart listing Advantages of Periodic Team Self-Evaluations (or hand out the sheet). Go over each item and make sure participants understand the value of having a team periodically review its progress as a team. Ask participants if they can think of other advantages. Ask if anyone has been a member or leader of a team that periodically rated its progress as a team. Ask for examples of how the evaluations were done and whether and why the evaluations were successful.

3. *Distribute and discuss the Team Health Questionnaire.* Explain that this is just one example of a questionnaire to help a team evaluate itself. Hand out pens or pencils. Divide participants into subgroups of four people each and give the subgroups the following assignment: Using the definition of "team health" arrived at earlier in the session, select the fifteen items from the questionnaire that would be *the most useful to a team when evaluating itself.* Allow about thirty minutes for this process. Tell the subgroups that it is important that they decide on *only* fifteen items during the time allowed.

4. *Discuss the process.* Bring the total group back together and lead a discussion of the process using the following questions:

   • What process did your subgroup use to select the fifteen items?

   • How successful was the process?

   • Did someone take a leadership role? How? What did the person do?

   • Are you happy with the fifteen items your subgroup selected? Why or why not?

   • What would you do differently if you had more time or could start over?

5. *Discuss how to conduct a team self-evaluation.* Hand out the Guidelines for a Team Self-Evaluation and discuss them with the group. Emphasize the importance of a *neutral* facilitator helping the team discuss its self-evaluation and deciding what it wants to improve on.

6. *Conduct team self-evaluations.* Instruct participants to return to the subgroups from the previous exercise. For the sake of time, ask each subgroup to evaluate itself on only the first fifteen items on the Team Health Questionnaire. Using those fifteen items, each subgroup should conduct a team self-evaluation as follows:

   a. Select one person from the subgroup to be a neutral facilitator.

   b. Have each person complete the first fifteen items on the Team Health Questionnaire. The ranking should be based on how the subgroup worked as a team in the previous exercise.

   c. The subgroup facilitator and a volunteer then tally the results and report back to the subgroup what the total responses were for each item.

   d. The facilitator asks what individuals think are the *strengths* of the subgroup, based on the results of the survey. The facilitator records these on a flip chart.

   e. The subgroup facilitator asks what individuals think are the *weaknesses* of the subgroup, based on the results of the survey. The facilitator records these on a flip chart.

   f. The subgroup facilitator then asks the subgroup what one or two actions it could take to improve its performance as a team. The facilitator records these on a flip chart.

7. *Debrief the activity.* After about thirty minutes, bring the subgroups back together and lead a discussion using the following questions:

   • How did the self-evaluation process go? What did you learn? What would you do differently next time?

   • What were some of the main *strengths* of your subgroups? What contributed to these strengths?

   • What were some of the *weaknesses*? What contributed to these weaknesses?

   • What action items did the subgroups select to improve performance as a team?

   • What were the advantages of having a neutral facilitator lead your subgroup discussion?

- If you were an ongoing team, how might you use this Team Health Questionnaire to improve your work as a team?

8. *Wrap up the session and adjourn.* Return to the goals for the session. Ask for feedback on the activity (see "Managing the Group Training Session: Tips for Trainers" in the Introduction, page 11) and adjourn.

ADVANTAGES OF PERIODIC TEAM SELF-EVALUATIONS

1. Team members and the team leader pause to think about how the team is operating as a team.

2. Team members and the team leader are given the opportunity to share opinions with one another about the effectiveness of the team.

3. Team members and the team leader share the responsibility for making improvements in how the team operates.

4. Problems can be targeted for improvement before they get out of hand.

5. Team members and the team leader know there is an avenue for addressing team problems.

6. Team members and the team leader can work together toward continual improvement as part of the natural process of teamwork.

TEAM HEALTH QUESTIONNAIRE

Instructions: Rank your team based on each of the items below. Circle *one* response for each item.

1. The long- and short-term goals of our team are clear to everyone on the team.

   Always Usually Seldom Never

2. Team members trust one another.

   Always Usually Seldom Never

3. All team members aim for the same team goals.

   Always Usually Seldom Never

4. Team members listen to one another and try to work collaboratively.

   Always Usually Seldom Never

5. The team leader draws on everyone's opinions and knowledge.

   Always Usually Seldom Never

6. Our team is clear about its boundaries, what the team's work is, and what it is not.

   Always Usually Seldom Never

7. Team members are linked so that one cannot succeed unless the others do, and vice versa.

   Always Usually Seldom Never

8. Our team holds regular team meetings that are well-run, stimulating, and productive.

   Always Usually Seldom Never

9. Team members are willing to share openly with one another if something is impacting the success of the team.

   Always Usually Seldom Never

10. Team members each carry a fair share of the team's workload.

    Always Usually Seldom Never

11. The team leader takes on the role of neutral facilitator when appropriate for the team's progress.

    Always Usually Seldom Never

12. Team members are free to express thoughts, feelings, ideas, and concerns without being ignored or put down.

    Always Usually Seldom Never

13. Team members feel they are in this together and that team members are not competing with one another.

           Always   Usually   Seldom   Never

14. Team members know each other, understand what one another's jobs are, and know whom to turn to for information or assistance.

           Always   Usually   Seldom   Never

15. Our team's achieves more than any one person could do alone.

           Always   Usually   Seldom   Never

16. Our team encourages and recognizes individual as well as team performance.

           Always   Usually   Seldom   Never

17. Working on the team is an enjoyable and satisfying experience.

           Always   Usually   Seldom   Never

18. Consensus is reached without sacrificing quality.

           Always   Usually   Seldom   Never

19. Team members and the team leader communicate dynamically and regularly with one another between team meetings.

           Always   Usually   Seldom   Never

20. Our team holds regular team meetings at which everyone is present, including the team leader.

           Always   Usually   Seldom   Never

21. Our team continually seeks to improve its performance by reviewing past problems and mistakes and taking action to correct them.

           Always   Usually   Seldom   Never

22. Team and individual action items and priorities are reviewed regularly and revised in a timely and appropriate manner.

           Always   Usually   Seldom   Never

23. Our team regularly develops plans, sets goals, and takes steps to achieve goals and implement its plans.

           Always   Usually   Seldom   Never

24. Our work is highly interdependent, and our tasks are linked.

           Always   Usually   Seldom   Never

25. Team members are clear about their individual roles, responsibilities, and authority.

           Always   Usually   Seldom   Never

26. Our team members and team leader communicate information effectively to those outside the team.

      Always   Usually   Seldom   Never

27. Decisions are made jointly through group participation with plenty of opportunity for input.

      Always   Usually   Seldom   Never

28. Our team has appropriate leadership and direction, and leaders are allowed to emerge from within the team.

      Always   Usually   Seldom   Never

29. Team members and the team leader periodically pause to evaluate how we are doing as a team.

      Always   Usually   Seldom   Never

30. Both individuals and the team as a whole are rewarded for their efforts.

      Always   Usually   Seldom   Never

31. Team members and the team leader are aware of each other's skills, competencies, and strengths.

      Always   Usually   Seldom   Never

32. People on the team are friendly and easy to approach; team members feel congenial toward one another.

      Always   Usually   Seldom   Never

GUIDELINES FOR A TEAM SELF-EVALUATION

1. Assign a neutral facilitator to oversee the process.

2. Allow team members time to complete the assessment individually and anonymously.

3. Tally the responses for each item.

4. Share the results of the survey with all the team members and team leader together.

5. Ask team members to determine one or two action steps they will take to improve their team, based on the survey.

6. Ask team members to agree on what else they want to do with the results of the survey.

Managing Growth
of a Team Leader

Purpose

- To begin a process for participants' own growth as team leaders
- To identify areas of strength and areas for improvement as team leaders
- To prioritize areas for improvement
- To identify *actions, resources,* and *methods* to increase skills, abilities, and confidence in those areas

Time

2 hours

Group Size

Designed for eight to twenty people

Materials

- Pencil, paper, and clipboard or other portable writing surface for each participant
- One Team Leader Self-Evaluation Form for each participant
- Up to ten copies of the Strategies for Development Worksheet per participant
- Flip chart and marking pens for the facilitator

Room Setup

A room large enough for participants to move about freely and confer with one another. Movable chairs should be available as well as plenty of wall space for posting flip charts.

Steps

1. *Give instructions for a pre-session activity.* Before the session begins, post the following two questions at the front of the room. As participants enter the room, give them paper and pencil and a clipboard (if necessary) and ask them to write down a few answers to the two questions:

   - What are some things you find particularly *frustrating* as a team leader?

   - What are some things that you find *motivating* and *encouraging* to you as a team leader?

2. *Introduce the goals of the session.* After reviewing the goals for the session, open the session with a brief discussion of the above questions. Allow a few more minutes for participants to write responses. Quickly and briefly record some of the responses on two separate flip charts posted in the front of the room. After about ten minutes, ask the group to summarize the comments they are hearing.

   Announce that the purpose of today's session is to give team leaders some self-evaluation and development tools so they can take charge of their own growth and development as team leaders. Say that team leaders make efforts to empower others and can also take the opportunity to empower themselves to develop skills and confidence as leaders. Mention that the process they will be using today can be repeated at various times throughout their work as team leaders. Their responses to the questions will help stimulate their thinking about areas of team leadership they can focus on.

   Mention that there are several areas to look at in relation to personal development in this area: one's role as a team leader, skills as a meeting facilitator, career in the organization, and work/life balance. Tell them that they will use a self-evaluation tool, discussions with others in the session, and their own insights to identify strengths and areas they would like to improve.

3. *Complete the Team Leader Self-Evaluation.* Distribute the Team Leader Self-Evaluation Form and ask participants to complete the form as honestly as possible. If they are not currently leading a team, ask them to imagine they have just been asked to lead a team at work and think about their current skill level in relation to the new assignments. Ask if there are any questions regarding completion of the form. Allow about ten minutes for everyone to complete the self-evaluation.

4. *Prioritize areas for improvement.* Next, instruct participants to prioritize the areas they indicated needed improvement or development, from most important (1) to least important (10). They may select as few as *five* or as many as *ten* priorities for improvement/development. Ask participants to write the numbers showing priority level in the column provided. Next, ask them to circle the top five strengths they already possess from the Doing Well column.

5. *Discuss results with partners.* Divide the group into pairs and ask each person to share his or her *five strengths* and *top five priorities for development* with his or her partner. Each person should select one area for development and brainstorm ideas with his or her partner as to how this area could be developed or improved. Allow about twenty minutes for partners to share and brainstorm.

6. *Complete the Strategies for Development Worksheet.* Ask each participant to find a private spot in which to begin to complete the worksheet. Suggest that they take their time and, if necessary, complete the worksheet after the session. Tell participants you will be available to brainstorm ideas with them as well. Allow at least thirty minutes for participants to think and write.

7. *Wrap up the session.* Bring the group back together. Ask participants to share some of the resource ideas they listed and post them on a flip chart for others to use, if they desire. If appropriate, have participants agree to a follow-up session within a specified time period (one or two months, for example), a time to discuss progress or setbacks, a time to get new ideas for development, and a time to renew their commitment to themselves. Set a time for the follow-up session.

8. *Review the goals for the session.* Ask for feedback on the activity (see "Managing the Group Training Session: Tips for Trainers" in the Introduction, page 11) and adjourn.

Variations

- Work with very small groups, such as four to six people. Provide time for participants to share their top priority items with the rest of the small group and have the groups brainstorm resources for development for each participant.

- Ask each partner to commit to supporting the other in some way (e.g., meet for coffee and discuss ideas, attend one another's team meeting and give feedback, attend a training program together, etc.).

TEAM LEADER SELF-EVALUATION FORM

Instructions: Rate each item on the form below according to what you think are your current skills and abilities in that area. Add any that you think are missing from this particular form and rate them as well. Place a checkmark in either Column I or Column II for each statement. In Column III, label your top five to ten priorities for improvement/development (1 = highest priority; 10 = lowest priority). If any of the statements do not apply in your situation, write NA after the statement and leave the columns blank. Save this evaluation for follow-up in a few weeks or months. You can complete it again in a few months, if desired.

Area for Potential Development	I. Doing Well	II. Would Like to Do Better	III. Priority for Development
Your Role as Team Leader			
Keep the team focused and on track			
Help team define its work boundaries			
Keep channels of communication open in the team			
Act as project manager for the team's projects			
Report team's progress to the organization/management			
Procure resources for the team (supplies, facilitator, budget, space, etc.)			
Clarify organization's expectations of the team			
Work with team members to ensure team productivity			
Contribute to the work of the team as a team member, without dominating or over-influencing			
Make sure team members are clear about decisions, action items, and commitments			
Help team resolve conflict			
Make sure team efforts are documented and made available, as needed, to the team or others			
Remove blocks and barriers to team success			
Defend the team's decisions to others in the organization			
Your Role as Meeting Leader for the Team			
Set up team meetings			
Develop results-oriented meeting objectives			
Design productive, interesting, and worthwhile team meetings			
Structure the meetings for maximum participation			
Remain neutral on the content, while taking an active role in the process of the meetings			

Area for Potential Development	I. Doing Well	II. Would Like to Do Better	III. Priority for Development
Suggest group processes that help the team do its best work			
Select from a variety of tools and processes, depending on the work the team is doing			
Ensure adequate follow-up on team meetings			
Draw out everyone and balance the participation			
Encourage dialogue among team members			
Record team members' ideas, decisions, and actions			
Listen actively to all team members			
Manage meeting time wisely			
Share the role of meeting leader with others			
Help team struggle through its conflicts and disagreements			
Create realistic meeting agendas			
Your "Career" and Role in the Organization			
Influence the larger organization			
Take an active role in the leadership of your organization			
Be a part of the direction your organization is heading			
Build a strong future for yourself in the organization			
Feel satisfied with the position and type of work you are doing			
Be part of a "support system" of other team leaders			
Feel supported and "mentored"			
Work/Life Balance			
Have an adequate balance of work and personal life			
Can separate work and personal life			
Am vitalized by my work (as opposed to being burned out)			
Can take off work when I really need to recharge my batteries, pursue enjoyable activities, or spend time with family/friends			
Have time to pursue a "healthy" lifestyle, if I so choose			
Put work in a realistic perspective; am not "consumed" by my work			
Can let go of a level of "perfection" at work so I can enjoy other things in life			

STRATEGIES FOR DEVELOPMENT WORKSHEET

Instructions: For each of your priorities for improvement/development, think about what you would like to achieve (your goal or vision for this area). Decide if there are any simple actions you can take to make progress, list strategies you can take, and identify resources you can look to for assistance. Recognize that some of these areas may be improved simply by your focusing attention on them and taking immediate action; others will have to be dealt with over the long term, since they may require experience, training, specific resources, or special effort on your part to change.

Priority _____

Brief description of the problem:

My goal/vision/wish for this area is (be as specific as possible):

Actions I could take immediately to make a difference (if any):

Longer-term strategies that will make a difference:

Resources that might help:

CONCLUSION

Becoming an effective team leader is an ongoing journey of which training activities are only a part. Part of any training strategy should be to help participants continually improve both their individual performance and the performance of their teams. For genuine growth to occur, team leaders must deepen their knowledge of concepts and enhance their skills *after* leaving the training. In addition to training, opportunities can be provided to support the ongoing development of the participants. For example, team leaders benefit greatly from the opportunity to discuss real-world challenges and victories with other team leaders in periodic get-togethers such as during lunch breaks or at brief monthly meetings.

Some of the activities in this book can be revisited from time to time and/or variations of them conducted as part of ongoing development. For example, Activity 23, *Solving Team Leader Challenges,* can be used over and over, focusing on different challenges each time. Once team leaders have completed Activity 19, *Resolving Conflict: A Consensus Process,* a follow-on session can be held for them to *practice* the consensus process using real situations from their experience. Activity 15, *Facilitation Practice for Team Leaders,* can be used as a springboard for continued learning; after the training, partners can be formed who attend one another's team meetings. After the meeting, they can get together to discuss what went well and what could be improved.

Other types of follow-on methods can be used to keep team leaders focused on their development. For example, following Activity 25, *Managing Growth of a Team Leader,* participants can be paired up and given the assignment of meeting together once a month to go over progress on their respective goals. A follow-up training session in a few months, bringing together the same participants, can be held to discuss how team leaders are progressing and to identify further training or support they need. Also, the training facilitator can hold a brief session with team leaders to brainstorm ideas for ongoing team leader get-togethers and development.

When deciding who should attend this team leader training, it is a good idea not to overlook *experienced* team leaders. Experienced as well as novice team leaders need training and ongoing development. Those with experience will assimilate even more of the training concepts and skills than they would if they were new to team leading. They are more apt to immediately use the training because they can more readily assess its value. Experienced team leaders may bring broader, more mature perspectives to training and are especially helpful in keeping those responsible for training focused on real-world applications. This is not to say that novice or less-experienced team leaders will not assimilate the training, but only to point out that training is valuable to experienced team leaders also.

In my work with team leaders, I have found them in general to be quick learners and ready to learn. They come to training with insightful questions and valid concerns and appreciate being supported in this way. Because most of them have already been members of teams, they relate easily to the topics and team-based learning approach. They have seen firsthand the importance of having an effective team leader on a team.

These activities are not "written in concrete." As you gain experience leading them, you will grow in facilitation experience as well as in knowledge of the audience with whom you are working. Over time, you will undoubtedly find ways to augment and adapt these exercises to enhance the learning for a particular audience. As facilitators of learning, you will learn along with the participants. Guiding team leaders on their developmental journey will give you ample opportunity to grow as a leader and facilitator as well.

ABOUT THE AUTHOR

FRAN REES is an experienced manager, consultant, and trainer in both the public and private sectors and the owner and principal consultant of Rees & Associates, a Phoenix-based training and consulting firm, which completed its eighteenth year in business in 2004.

Ms. Rees has designed and led workshops in management development, teamwork, facilitation, presentation, work force diversity, and internal consulting. She has consulted to a variety of industries and organizations, including computer manufacturing, health care, city and state governments, biomedical technology, utilities, and food production. Much of her current work focuses on team development, team leadership, and team facilitation.

She is the author of four other books: a publisher's bestseller, *How to Lead Work Teams: Facilitation Skills* (2nd ed.) (2001), *Teamwork from Start to Finish* (1997), *The Facilitator Excellence Handbook* (1998), and *Facilitator Excellence Instructor Guide* (1998), all published by Pfeiffer. *How to Lead Work Teams* has been published in Spanish and Polish, and *The Facilitator Excellence Handbook* was recently published in Japanese.

Ms. Rees' L.E.A.D. model of leadership, her books, and her workshops are used in a variety of settings to develop team leaders, guide self-managed teams, and train facilitators.

Pfeiffer Publications Guide

This guide is designed to familiarize you with the various types of Pfeiffer publications. The formats section describes the various types of products that we publish; the methodologies section describes the many different ways that content might be provided within a product. We also provide a list of the topic areas in which we publish.

FORMATS

In addition to its extensive book-publishing program, Pfeiffer offers content in an array of formats, from fieldbooks for the practitioner to complete, ready-to-use training packages that support group learning.

FIELDBOOK Designed to provide information and guidance to practitioners in the midst of action. Most fieldbooks are companions to another, sometimes earlier, work, from which its ideas are derived; the fieldbook makes practical what was theoretical in the original text. Fieldbooks can certainly be read from cover to cover. More likely, though, you'll find yourself bouncing around following a particular theme, or dipping in as the mood, and the situation, dictate.

HANDBOOK A contributed volume of work on a single topic, comprising an eclectic mix of ideas, case studies, and best practices sourced by practitioners and experts in the field.

An editor or team of editors usually is appointed to seek out contributors and to evaluate content for relevance to the topic. Think of a handbook not as a ready-to-eat meal, but as a cookbook of ingredients that enables you to create the most fitting experience for the occasion.

RESOURCE Materials designed to support group learning. They come in many forms: a complete, ready-to-use exercise (such as a game); a comprehensive resource on one topic (such as conflict management) containing a variety of methods and approaches; or a collection of like-minded activities (such as icebreakers) on multiple subjects and situations.

TRAINING PACKAGE An entire, ready-to-use learning program that focuses on a particular topic or skill. All packages comprise a guide for the facilitator/trainer and a workbook for the participants. Some packages are supported with additional media—such as video—or learning aids, instruments, or other devices to help participants understand concepts or practice and develop skills.

- *Facilitator/trainer's guide* Contains an introduction to the program, advice on how to organize and facilitate the learning event, and step-by-step instructor notes. The guide also contains copies of presentation materials—handouts, presentations, and overhead designs, for example—used in the program.

- *Participant's workbook* Contains exercises and reading materials that support the learning goal and serves as a valuable reference and support guide for participants in the weeks and months that follow the learning event. Typically, each participant will require his or her own workbook.

ELECTRONIC CD-ROMs and web-based products transform static Pfeiffer content into dynamic, interactive experiences. Designed to take advantage of the searchability, automation, and ease-of-use that technology provides, our e-products bring convenience and immediate accessibility to your workspace.

METHODOLOGIES

CASE STUDY A presentation, in narrative form, of an actual event that has occurred inside an organization. Case studies are not prescriptive, nor are they used to prove a point; they are designed to develop critical analysis and decision-making skills. A case study has a specific time frame, specifies a sequence of events, is narrative in structure, and contains a plot structure—an issue (what should be/have been done?). Use case studies when the goal is to enable participants to apply previously learned theories to the circumstances in the case, decide what is pertinent, identify the real issues, decide what should have been done, and develop a plan of action.

ENERGIZER A short activity that develops readiness for the next session or learning event. Energizers are most commonly used after a break or lunch to stimulate or refocus the group. Many involve some form of physical activity, so they are a useful way to counter post-lunch lethargy. Other uses include transitioning from one topic to another, where "mental" distancing is important.

EXPERIENTIAL LEARNING ACTIVITY (ELA) A facilitator-led intervention that moves participants through the learning cycle from experience to application (also known as a Structured Experience). ELAs are carefully thought-out designs in which there is a definite learning purpose and intended outcome. Each step—everything that participants do during the activity—facilitates the accomplishment of the stated goal. Each ELA includes complete instructions for facilitating the intervention and a clear statement of goals, suggested group size and timing, materials required, an explanation of the process, and, where appropriate, possible variations to the activity. (For more detail on Experiential Learning Activities, see the Introduction to the *Reference Guide to Handbooks and Annuals*, 1999 edition, Pfeiffer, San Francisco.)

GAME A group activity that has the purpose of fostering team sprit and togetherness in addition to the achievement of a pre-stated goal. Usually contrived—undertaking a desert expedition, for example—this type of learning method offers an engaging means for participants to demonstrate and practice business and interpersonal skills. Games are effective for team building and personal development mainly because the goal is subordinate to the process—the means through which participants reach decisions, collaborate, communicate, and generate trust and understanding. Games often engage teams in "friendly" competition.

ICEBREAKER A (usually) short activity designed to help participants overcome initial anxiety in a training session and/or to acquaint the participants with one another. An icebreaker can be a fun activity or can be tied to specific topics or training goals. While a useful tool in itself, the icebreaker comes into its own in situations where tension or resistance exists within a group.

INSTRUMENT A device used to assess, appraise, evaluate, describe, classify, and summarize various aspects of human behavior. The term used to describe an instrument depends primarily on its format and purpose. These terms include survey, questionnaire, inventory, diagnostic, survey, and poll. Some uses of instruments include providing instrumental feedback to group members, studying here-and-now processes or functioning within a group, manipulating group composition, and evaluating outcomes of training and other interventions.

Instruments are popular in the training and HR field because, in general, more growth can occur if an individual is provided with a method for focusing specifically on his or her own behavior. Instruments also are used to obtain information that will serve as a basis for change and to assist in workforce planning efforts.

Paper-and-pencil tests still dominate the instrument landscape with a typical package comprising a facilitator's guide, which offers advice on administering the instrument and interpreting the collected data, and an initial set of instruments. Additional instruments are available separately. Pfeiffer, though, is investing heavily in e-instruments. Electronic instrumentation provides effortless distribution and, for larger groups particularly, offers advantages over paper-and-pencil tests in the time it takes to analyze data and provide feedback.

LECTURETTE A short talk that provides an explanation of a principle, model, or process that is pertinent to the participants' current learning needs. A lecturette is intended to establish a common language bond between the trainer and the participants by providing a mutual frame of reference. Use a lecturette as an introduction to a group activity or event, as an interjection during an event, or as a handout.

MODEL A graphic depiction of a system or process and the relationship among its elements. Models provide a frame of reference and something more tangible, and more easily remembered, than a verbal explanation. They also give participants something to "go on," enabling them to track their own progress as they experience the dynamics, processes, and relationships being depicted in the model.

ROLE PLAY A technique in which people assume a role in a situation/scenario: a customer service rep in an angry-customer exchange, for example. The way in which the role is approached is then discussed and feedback is offered. The role play is often repeated using a different approach and/or incorporating changes made based on feedback received. In other words, role playing is a spontaneous interaction involving realistic behavior under artificial (and safe) conditions.

SIMULATION A methodology for understanding the interrelationships among components of a system or process. Simulations differ from games in that they test or use a model that depicts or mirrors some aspect of reality in form, if not necessarily in content. Learning occurs by studying the effects of change on one or more factors of the model. Simulations are commonly used to test hypotheses about what happens in a system—often referred to as "what if?" analysis—or to examine best-case/worst-case scenarios.

THEORY A presentation of an idea from a conjectural perspective. Theories are useful because they encourage us to examine behavior and phenomena through a different lens.

TOPICS

The twin goals of providing effective and practical solutions for workforce training and organization development and meeting the educational needs of training and human resource professionals shape Pfeiffer's publishing program. Core topics include the following:

Leadership & Management

Communication & Presentation

Coaching & Mentoring

Training & Development

e-Learning

Teams & Collaboration

OD & Strategic Planning

Human Resources

Consulting

What will you find on pfeiffer.com?

- The best in workplace performance solutions for training and HR professionals

- Downloadable training tools, exercises, and content

- Web-exclusive offers

- Training tips, articles, and news

- Seamless on-line ordering

- Author guidelines, information on becoming a Pfeiffer Affiliate, and much more

Discover more at www.pfeiffer.com

Customer Care

Have a question, comment, or suggestion? Contact us! We value your feedback and we want to hear from you.

For questions about this or other Pfeiffer products, you may contact us by:

E-mail: **customer@wiley.com**

Mail: **Customer Care Wiley/Pfeiffer**
10475 Crosspoint Blvd.
Indianapolis, IN 46256

Phone: **(US) 800-274-4434** (Outside the US: 317-572-3985)

Fax: **(US) 800-569-0443** (Outside the US: 317-572-4002)

To order additional copies of this title or to browse other Pfeiffer products, visit us online at **www.pfeiffer.com**.

For **Technical Support** questions call **(800) 274-4434.**

For author guidelines, log on to www.pfeiffer.com and click on "Resources for Authors."

If you are . . .

A **college bookstore, a professor, an instructor, or work in higher education** and you'd like to place an order or request an exam copy, please contact jbreview@wiley.com.

A **general retail bookseller** and you'd like to establish an account or speak to a local sales representative, contact Melissa Grecco at 201-748-6267 or mgrecco@wiley.com.

An **exclusively on-line bookseller**, contact Amy Blanchard at 530-756-9456 or ablanchard @wiley.com or Jennifer Johnson at 206-568-3883 or jjohnson@wiley.com, both of our Online Sales department.

A **librarian or library representative**, contact John Chambers in our Library Sales department at 201-748-6291 or jchamber@wiley.com.

A **reseller, training company/consultant, or corporate trainer**, contact Charles Regan in our Special Sales department at 201-748-6553 or cregan@wiley.com.

A **specialty retail distributor** (includes specialty gift stores, museum shops, and corporate bulk sales), contact Kim Hendrickson in our Special Sales department at 201-748-6037 or khendric@wiley.com.

Purchasing for the **Federal government**, contact Ron Cunningham in our Special Sales department at 317-572-3053 or rcunning@wiley.com.

Purchasing for a **State or Local government**, contact Charles Regan in our Special Sales department at 201-748-6553 or cregan@wiley.com.